From Khizanat Al-Adab, Cairo, Al-Matbaa Al-Asriyah 1870

ARABLIT QUARTERLY

VOLUME 2, ISSUE 2
SUMMER 2019

Editor-in-chief: M Lynx Qualey
Art Director: Hassân Al Mohtasib
Contributing Editors: Nashwa Gowanlock,
Sawad Hussain, and Lara Vergnaud

A production of www.arablit.org
Opinions, submissions, advertising:
info@arablit.org

ب – ح – ر

◆

Ba–Ha–Ra:
the root for sea, vastness, depth ...

◆

Table of Contents

VOLUME 2, ISSUE 2, SUMMER 2019

٢
/
2

Fisherman's boat on the lake, Tiberias, Holy Land, between ca. 1890 and ca. 1900
Library of Congress Prints and Photographs Division

INTRODUCTION

FEATURES

POETRY

SHORT FICTION

TRANSLATE THIS!

FOOD FOR READING

$\frac{\varepsilon}{4}$

Introduction

Ahmad Faris al-Shidyaq did not love the sea.

It was March of 1826 when his brother As'ad was arrested on the orders of Lebanon's Maronite patriarch on charges of heresy. The great author- and translator-to-be, then 20 or 21, sought refuge with his elder brother's Protestant missionary friends. It was almost 30 years later that al-Shidyaq wrote about his first, disastrous sea journey in *Leg over Leg*. There, in his demi-autobiographical narrative, he describes how the missionaries thought it best to send him off to the "Island of Scoundrels"—that is, Malta—and how they put him on a ship headed for Alexandria.

أحمد فارس الشدياق
Leg over Leg

مارون

By M Lynx Qualey

The ship hasn't gone far when the sea rises, and al-Shidyaq's fictional alter ego grows sick and dizzy. What follows is a long "lament and plaint" upon the sea. As the narrator considers his predicament, the "ship gave him a violent shove," and he begins to rant about the events that have brought him to this point. In Humphrey Davies' translation: "This cry had barely left his lips before the ship gave a list to one side that sent his little head rolling like a watermelon," after which he yells for help. Finally, the sea grows calm, and the safety of the Alexandrine shore appears on the horizon.

Al-Shidyaq's protagonist is the first passenger to elbow his way off the ship and back on to dry land, and "no sooner had he set foot on the ground than he picked up some pebbles from its surface and swallowed them, declaring, 'This is my mother and to it I return. On it I was born and on it I shall die.'"

Although he travels many more times, al-Shidyaq remains firmly a dry-ground man, a satirist rather than a romantic. Much of Arabic literature, however, is deeply entwined with the rhythms of the sea. The bahr is, after all, not just a word that points to the sea, but also to poetic meter. In the prose-poetic *In the Presence of Absence,* Mahmoud Darwish's words sway back and forth with the steadying rhythms of the sea. Darwish writes that words are waves, and that the sea— "imprisoned in three letters, the second of which overflows with salt"—is the mother of rhythm. In Sinan Antoon's translation: "Teach me poetry. Teach me the rhythm of the sea."

But if for Darwish the sea represents a deep sonic love, and for al-Shidyaq it's a wretched marriage of convenience, for many Arabic-language writers, it's complicated. The sea is adventure and travel. It is romance, waves, and summer beaches. But it is also loss and exile. It is the Mediterranean that has eaten the bodies of so many children.

In Nazik al-Malaika's 1974 "And We Still Have the Sea," translated here by Emily Drumsta, there is romance and power, but also drowning, exile, and death. Al-Malaika was born in 1923 and finished a Master's in comparative literature at the landlocked University of Wisconsin-Madison in 1959, two years before Joyce Carol-Oates received her M.A. from the same institution. Al-Malaika returned to Iraq, where army officers had recently overthrown the monarchy and established a republic. Through the 1960s, there followed a series of coups and counter-coups, as well as a war between governmental and Kurdish forces. Saddam Hussein came to power in 1968; the First Kurdish Iraq War ended in 1970; and, in that same year, al-Malaika and her family packed up and left the country for Kuwait. She never again lived in Iraq.

The poem she wrote four years later begins with a question.

Its narrator is asked about the sea, "do its colors change?" and they respond, "yes, / my love / the sea changes colors / green ships surge across it / pale cities emerge from it / and sometimes it drinks the sunset's blood[.]" Yet the sea is not only shades of green, blue, and red, but sometimes, "my love, it changes and turns the color of ash / and tastes just like a sleepless night / all of its fish are ash" and "domes of sunken cities ash, and the face of a drowned man / floating, pillowed on the salty waves, unconscious, is ash-colored[.]"

Ahmed Naji's "I Bit My Tail & It Tasted So Good" takes place in an alternate reality where the sea is a violent border. An electrified steel fence is erected to separate the North Mediterranean countries from those of the South. Detention camps are established all along the coast, where the organs of the imprisoned can be traded for freedom, such that a donated kidney can gain you the funds to buy a food cart. "Of course, after a month of happily standing in front of the liver cart, in this situation that has been brought about through the slavery of your employment, the police come to cite your cart for violating regulations in using a deep-fat fryer in a public space as set forth in the Paris Accords on Climate Change and Global Warming, and the cycle of your unhappiness begins again."

Sometimes the sea appears, in this issue of ArabLit Quarterly, in its other meanings (as a sea of light, a sea of languages). But throughout this issue—our third—we swing back and forth between the sea as a site of pleasure and one of shocking violence. After all, another cluster of meanings for بحر is "slit, cut, or divided lengthwise; split; or clave; and enlarged; or made wide." The Orientalist Edward William Lane, perhaps erroneously, relays that he's heard an origin story for the word بحر wherein the word that means both "sea" and "great river" comes from a terrific rent in the earth that is filled with life-giving water. The sea is thus a wound that has been filled in by beauty; a wound nonetheless. ◆

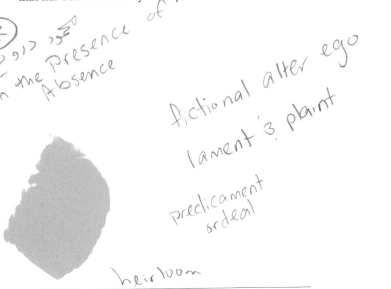

And...

…We Still Have the Sea

By **Nazik al-Mala'ika**

we stood by the sea in the midday heat, two excited kids
my spirit swimming through your fields
      the flooded rivers of your eyes
my heart running after a question
whose buds perfume your lips

Translated by
Emily Drumsta

your question is a sweet north wind
the beauty of a song poured from lovesick violins
hidden in your hands
your question shines sky-colored onto trellises and ponds
you asked about the sea, do its colors change?
are its waves different shades? do its shores shift?

you asked, with your eyes wide as dreams
your face a distant star
lost ships without a harbor
you asked, your lashes ears of wheat
a field that swells in waves, the wonder of a child
your hands the flowing sails
on two boats
driven out beyond the distance, beyond what we can see
and I said, yes,
my love
the sea changes colors
green ships surge across it
pale cities emerge from it
and sometimes it drinks the sunset's blood
and sometimes it turns the color of sky
gathering its blue, my love
and dreaming, gazing with scattered
celestial eyes
into endlessness, turning the color of light
in the morning, dimming its chandelier at night
you asked about the sea, do its colors change?
are its waves different shades? do its shorelines shift?
yes, my love,
a sea laps at the edges of my soul's ravine
passing through harbors of color and sun
and deserted fields
a moonlit twilight bathes in its waves
wetting its hair
tossing down a portion of its twinkling sky
yes, my love, and the sea also colors its gulfs
yes, the sea changes colors
it drinks up the yellow of my doubt and distrust
it takes on the blue color of my melody
as my songs and ships set sail on its scattered waves
it turns white, its seafloor jasmine-colored
it turns green, like the green of sad eyes
like the peridot waters of Nahavand
in the depths of my grief.

you asked about the sea, do its colors change?
your eyes are a sea, vast
            shores lost
yes, my love, the sea changes its colors and turns ashy-grey
and tastes just like a night when sleep stayed far away
all of its fish are ash, its pearls
ash
            sponges
            octopuses ash
domes of sunken cities ash, and the face of a drowned man
floating, pillowed on the salty waves, unconscious, is ash-colored
swallowing water, the salt nightshade and ash on his lips
my ocean, your ocean, this ocean of ash
has a loving heart
and a harshness that slaps at the corpse, spreading out, pillow-soft
quarreling with the drowned gray body, my sea and your sea
            sent its violent wave to strike him
and mermaids who bore him
            to sands of forgetting like wine
he lies on the shore, senseless, inert
            and the sea of ash
sprays his motionless form, and a wave of love
plays on his cheeks and washes his face till
it glistens with love and salt and foam
                        sometimes covering the body
sometimes returning, retreating, leaving it
to numb eternity

you who ask me:
            does my sea and your sea change colors?
does it paint its shores in oils and coal like the clouds?
my love, when I was little my grandfather
was tall and long like hair braided in spring
he had depth
            shadow
                        distance
and the violence of an autumn storm
he was wise as a magical, edgeless sea
and strong as a wave

one day tongues of flame came to our house
to gnaw at the walls and set curtains alight
the flames turned in circles
roaring on the balconies of our dreams, laughing at our terror
threatening to spread, running through our neighborhood
vowing to devour cheeks
                                lips
                                     doors
and even the boys on the threshing-floors

my grandfather rushed at it, as rash as a wave
and with a cry of fright
fell upon it with a tornado's violence, cursing and railing
his insults rain and longing, his ferocity a melodious line of verse,
a whispered prayer, a morning star
a perfumed boat
the abuse on his lips a colorful stream
and my grandfather put out the fire
saving my lashes and hair

my love—my grandfather was an ocean
changing colors, turning the quarries of his eyes black and green
changing waves, reaching into the distance, forming pearls
making springs flow, mooring on shores
creating space, sculpting islands
scattering golden islands across the gulf's blue
and his buckets full of curses were vials of balm
breaking bracelets of fire from forearms and wrists

the strength of the waves in my sea and your sea
has transformed into hands and a chest
to bear up the body of the drowned man
rain down kisses and love
and lay it gently on safety's shores
with the fluttering wings of a dove

and give him new life
        sow his death with dreams
               and memory's wheat
and the cold of a cloud
how can you ask me about color and the sea, my love,
when you are my sail
        and the colors of my sea
               and the dreaminess in my eyes
when you are the mist on my paths
my canvas
        when you are the peaks of my waves
my sad rose, my pale perfume?

you ask me about color and the sea, my love
but you are my seas
my pearl and my shell
and your face is my home
so carry my boat on a wave of desire, hidden, enclosed
to a dark and impossible shore
        with no flatlands, no hills
to a twilight with moonlit expanses
deep
colorless in the light of day
branchless in the forest's thick
free of terror, free of hope

we'll lose ourselves there
eating the warmth of winter, plucking the snow of spring
praising frost's wool
where the shadows are shapeless
where fate has no ledger
and a glance raises nothing
but the wave of a song coming down
through the moon's mountains

we laugh we cry your eyes
reflect the color of the sea
we still have color
               sea
                     eternity.

Illustrations: Hassán Al Mohtasib

Taleb al-Refai's shipwreck-novel *Najdi* was longlisted for the 2018 International Prize for Arabic Fiction and is forthcoming in French translation. It follows the last days in the life of one of Kuwait's most famous sea captains, Ali al-Najdi, who appears as a character in Alan Villiers' 1940 *Sons of Sindbad*.

Najdi

By **Taleb al-Refai**

Translated by
Russell Harris

Youtube

What moments in your own life brought you to writing this book? How has your relationship with the sea changed as the country's relationship with it has changed?

Taleb al-Refai: The novel is a conversation that once passed through my head when I was a child sitting on the beach and listening to the waves telling stories. I spent my childhood in an old area of Kuwait called "Sharq," which was the same area where my protagonist Ali al-Najdi lived. The coastline was shared by me and my hero, although he was born in 1900; I was born in 1958.

Before the discovery and export of oil in 1946, and the discovery of artificial pearls in the mid-1940s, Kuwaitis lived from pearl diving in the summer and trade with Africa and India in the winter. I'm from a generation that did not know the life of the sea. When I was born, Kuwait had started living a modern urban life. The concrete houses, the asphalt streets, and all the state institutions were in process. From that time, the Kuwaitis have lived with the sea as a form of leisure and pleasure.

In terms of textual rhythms, did writing about the sea changed how you worked?

TaR: I wrote about the sea as a character and influential personality, and this writing created its vocabulary, internal music, and the speed of its flow. In the novel, there are two levels of the writing: the first level comes before the storm and takes the shape of flashbacks, including various memories and stories. The second level comes after the storm. It comes in very short sentences, echoing the crazy storm, rain, wind, and darkness.

Do you have favorite sea novels? Sea poetry? Sea chants or songs?

TaR: There are a lot of poems and short stories written about the sea by Kuwaiti poets and novelists, in addition to a great heritage of Kuwaiti maritime singing. The film "The Cruel Sea," directed by Kuwaiti director Khalid Siddiq, is also one of my favorites.

What sort of research did you do into sea songs, prayers, historical trade routes, storms, Ali's life, pearl diving?

TaR: I spent more than a year researching the historical relationship between the Kuwaitis and the sea: shipbuilding in Kuwait, marine singing, pearl diving, and the seasons for travel. I took special care with the life of Captain Ali al-Najdi, and I met with his sons and grandsons, having many conversations with Nasser Husain Ali Alnajdi. When I finished writing the novel, I presented it to the historian and writer Dr. Yaghob Al-Ghunaim and the maritime historian Dr. Yaghob al-Hajji. But many of the historical practices in the novel are part of Kuwait's indigenous knowledge, easy to access in any household.

If you were to return to write another sea novel, what sort of novel would it be?

TaR: It would be a story about the lives of Kuwaiti women and would shed the light on how women ran things while men spent four months pearl diving, then returned home, spending nearly a month in Kuwait before they returned to their boats, heading to the shores of East Africa and India for another four months or so. In the absence of men, women did everything (humanitarian, administrative, and financial) under very difficult conditions, amidst a community of men, amidst the cruelty of nature.

10:30 p.m.

We are now some distance from where the yacht capsized. When the storm dies down, lights will appear along the coast, reassuring us, and the outline of the coast will grow clear. For sailors, light is life.

I am not going to lose Kuwait.
I hope the storm won't last much longer.
"How long has the storm been going?" Sulayman asks me.
"It started up at ten. About half an hour."
"How long do you think it will keep on?" Abd al-Wahab asks.
"God knows." I sigh.
Our rigid fingers clutch the edge of the bobbing fish crate.
Our bodies are submerged in the water, and the black waves strike us from all sides.
"I'm going to die." I can hear Abd al-Wahab moaning through the darkness.
"Just think of God, my brother," Sulayman barks back at him.
"The storm's going to die down."

"My dishdasha's soaked, and it's pulling me down."
"We'll get it off you," Sulayman says. "Hold tight to the crate."
"Ali and I are going to try and get you out of it."
Abd al-Wahab will be like me and Sulayman, naked except for his long underwear.
"We'll rip it open at the neckline. That'll make it easier to get it off you," I shout at Abd al-Wahab. He agrees.
We're talking into the darkness. We speak without seeing each other's faces.
I think of my ogal and remove it. It can be used as a rope. I raise my voice and address Abd al-Wahab: "Don't let go of the crate. I'm going to tie my ogal around your wrist, so hold on to it while Sulayman gets your dishdasha off you."
The crate is bobbing wildly with the waves, trying to shake us off. I grab Abd al-Wahab's wrist and feel him giving me his arm. I wind the cord firmly around it.
"Sulayman," I say, still unable to see anything. "I've secured Abd al-Wahab's arm and I'm holding onto him. Get his dishdasha off him."
The cold air slaps our faces with rain.
Sulayman is pulling his brother's dishdasha off him as we're tossed around with the crate.

"God give me strength!" Sulayman calls out at he pulls the dishdasha off Abd al-Wahab's compliant body. One end of the cord is around his arm, and the other is looped around my hand.
"Grab the neckline of his dishdasha," I tell Sulayman.
"We'll each pull in our own direction."
Why, O sea?
I told my father, "The sea's my friend." My mother said: "What a load of nonsense!"
I let go of Abd al-Wahab's hand and shout to him: "Hold tight to the crate!"
I grope around for the neck of his dishdasha and tell Sulayman: "Let's pull on it together. You to your side, me to mine."
When sailors tug on the rigging, they do so as one man.
I stretch out my hand to feel for the dishdasha's neck opening. I cannot see Abd al-Wahab's face. I grab the front of his dishdasha.

"Pull!" I shout at Sulayman, and I tug hard on the dishdasha. The crate wobbles, and Abd al-Wahab moves towards me. The neckline of the dishdasha starts to rip. That's a bad omen, I tell myself.

"Slide your arm out," Sulayman yells at his brother Abd al-Wahab. The cold is starting to grip my shoulders, neck and head. My back hurts from when I fell.

"God have mercy on us!" Abd al-Wahab pleads. He leans against the crate as he yanks his arm out of its sleeve. The edge of the crate is going under.

"Don't worry about the crate," I tell him, feeling for the ogal wrapped around his arm. If Abd al-Wahab lets go of the crate, he'll drown.

"I can't get my other arm out." Abd al-Wahab's voice pleads with me.

The heavy, sodden winter dishdasha is pulling us down into the deep.

"I'm going to slip the cord off your wrist. Hold tight to the crate with your other hand. Then I'll be able to get you out of the dishdasha."

I slide the ogal off while trying to keep Abd al-Wahab close. I slip the cord around my neck so I don't lose it.

The storm is still in the depths of its madness, and there is nothing but darkness, rain, and waves, and the weight of the winter dishdasha on my arm. Noura said: "You're not as young as you used to be." I try to free Abd al-Wahab's arm from the dishdasha.

The crate wobbles. I get the dishdasha off his shoulder and feel it slide off him.

"Get your hand out of it!" I yell. The dishdasha comes off. I let go, and it disappears into the darkness of the sea.

Abd al-Wahab is now wearing only his long underwear. The black waves slam into us from all directions.

"Keep hold of the crate," I tell Abd al-Wahab.

"What are we doing to do?" His question blurs into the darkness.

"We're going to hold onto the crate until the storm has passed."

"We'll die of hypothermia," he says in despair.

"We're not going to die. I spent a whole night on the lifeboat al-Mashaw."

"Enough about death," Sulayman objects. "It's a storm. It'll pass."

"An hour ago, the sea was calm—"

"We should've headed back earlier," Sulayman interrupts me with his lament.

"I asked you two…" But I swallow the rest of my sentence.

I'm not going to blame anyone. "It's my fault."

"It's the will of God, my brother," Sulayman says, clearly trying to make me feel better.

The storm is growing stronger. The waves are even higher, and we cling to the crate that was thrown free of the yacht. Cold rain hammers down on our heads.

"All we have left is the mercy of God," Abd al-Wahab says.

"We've just got to keep hold of the crate until the storm dies down," Sulayman tells him.

"And when's that going to be?" Abd al-Wahab asks again.

"Not long. These storms come from nowhere and disappear."

Abd al-Wahab once told a gathering of men: "When I'm with the nakhoda, the captain, I don't have to think about anything." He was talking about his sea voyages, showing how much trust he had in me. "Ali is a creature of the sea!"

Oh, Abd al-Wahab. That nakhoda, that creature of the sea, is now dangling in the darkness while clutching a fish crate.

The wind is growing stronger. I don't think it will calm down any time soon, but I keep that to myself.

You have lived through many trials on the sea, Ali. But you weren't old then.

"The storm will pass, and we'll be rescued," I yell out, as if addressing myself.

"If we swim holding on to the crate, which way should we head?" Sulayman asks me.

"We're near Jelieh." I look up at the sky, and the darkness and water fall down into my eyes, suffocating me. The storm is trying to test me. I have the coastline in my head: "The moment the storm stops, we'll be able to head towards the shore," I tell Sulayman.

"But when?" Abd al-Wahab repeats his irritating question, and I ignore it.

The sky seizes our breath, suffocating us. Only our heads are above water, and they are battered by the rain and the wind.

O Lord, if you want to take one of us, take me. I am Ali bin Nasser al-Najdi. How will I be able to face the people of Kuwait? Let me have an honourable death. Dear God, don't humiliate me in my old age.

My father said: "The sea befriends no one."

Yet I was not expecting a treacherous storm in the middle of February.

I know these dark moments. Every lifetime has its moment, and every such moment brings death.

"I've started shivering from the cold," Abd al-Wahab complains.

"Don't weaken, my brother," I tell him, adding: "If you weaken, you'll take us with you."

"Stay strong, brother!" Sulayman calls out.

I am afraid that Abd al-Wahab will drown. I'll re-tie the cord around his arm, fixing the other end to the handle of the crate. If his body gives up, or he no longer has the strength to hold on, he'll still be attached to the crate. I unwind the ogal from my neck.

"Give me your arm," I tell him. Between us, there is only darkness and rain. The waves toss around the crate, and us along with it.

"I'm going to tie your arm to the handle."

"No." He rejects the idea. "If I drown, I'll pull the crate down with me."

"There won't be any drowning," I growl.

We shout at each other blindly in the darkness as I grope around for his arm. His right arm is hanging on to the crate. Somehow, I will wrap the ogal around his arm.

"You have to come over towards the handle," I tell him, and add quickly to Sulayman: "We've got to turn the crate so that the handle is close to Abd al-Wahab."

Abd al-Wahab is out there in the darkness, giving up the ghost. Why, Ali, do you shout at Abd al-Wahab when he is paralysed by fear and fatigue?

The wind is howling around us.

"Hang on," Sulayman says. "The storm is growing stronger."

The crate sways as we hold it, filling up with water.

I'm holding the end of the cord so I can tie it to the handle. I don't want my friend Abd al-Wahab to drown. We haven't seen another yacht or boat since we arrived. But even if a boat were to pass by, no one would see or hear us.

"How long are we going to be out here?" Abd al-Wahab returns to his painful question.

"The storm will die down," I say.

"Look!" Sulayman's voice calls out from the darkness.

"A light. A float—a buoy!"

I focus in on it. "That's the marker for the district of Jelieh."

"God be praised," Sulayman shouts with delight, and adds: "Let's try and get over to it."

"It's far."

"We can swim towards it," Sulayman says enthusiastically.

I feel for the movement of the waves and wind. In what direction will it be easiest to swim? How will Sulayman manage to reach the marker in all this wind and rain and swell?

"You have to swim this way," I yell, drawing an arc in the direction of the wind, but the darkness swallows up my gesture. I shout at him: "It's not going to be an easy swim."

"I'm going to let go of the crate and swim," Sulayman shouts.

"Keep the marker in your sight," I tell him. "We're going to be right behind you."

"Here I go," Abd al-Wahab says.

O God, treat him kindly!

"Are you up to swimming?" I ask. "Wait. I'll undo the ogal."

My hand fumbles around for the cord.

"Aren't you coming with us?" Sulayman asks.

"I'm going to keep hold of the crate and swim behind you. If either of you gets tired, swim back toward me."

"If we can get onto the marker, come with us."

"The important thing is you save yourselves," I shout.

Abd al-Wahab's hand is now free. I reach out to grab Sulayman's hands.

"Stay strong."

"God protect us," he says despondently.

The black waves are tossing the crate around more than ever. "Let go of the crate one at a time," I tell them. "And swim close to each other."

The waves, the wind and the darkness might separate them.

"We'll swim together. Swim close to me," Sulayman warns Abd al-Wahab.

I look towards the light on the marker. From this distance, I can see it moving up and down. It will be difficult to climb onto the marker. The sharp barnacles and coral growing on it will slash anyone who tries to climb up, and the smell of blood will attract sharks.

"I'll be close to you, holding on to the crate."

"I put my trust in God," Sulayman says as he lets go of the crate. No doubt he hears me uttering, "Forgive me, friend."

Abd al-Wahab follows, and I can make out Sulayman's voice saying,

"You're forgiven, Ali."

The black sky clings to my head, and I'm alone with the movements of the crate, which is tossing me around.

They have swum off a little, and I cannot make out their bodies in the darkness.

I paddle with one hand in order to stay near them. I'm worried about Abd al-Wahab.

The crate thrashes around, trying to throw me off.

I paddle with one hand. The crate does not want to do my bidding. I must not be far from them. I have to follow. The light of the marker appears, and then disappears. It's not close. The wind is playing with it, and it's going to be difficult to climb on. The hard surface of the buoy will smash into anyone who tries to get close.

I am alone out here, hanging on to the mad crate. I cannot make out any movement from the two men. The marker is still far away. I am paddling, but the waves are against me.

The sea has betrayed me. I misjudged it. I should have trusted my sense of foreboding and the foul smell.

The darkness and the waves hide everything. Where is Abd al-Wahab?

If I paddled more furiously, I might reach him. I can't let him drown. But I'm starting to feel fatigued.

"God!" I shout, but the waves swallow my entreaty.

Where is Abd al-Wahab? I shout to him: "Abd al-Wahab!" I can sense him nearby.
"Abd al-Wahab!"
I think I hear a voice, but it's the roar of the waves and the rain.
"Abd al-Wahab!" I strain to hear a response.
"Ali," I hear him reply. Abd al-Wahab is still alive. I look around me in all directions,
but my eyes are blinded by the darkness.
"Abd al-Wahab!" I shout at the top of my voice.
"Yes." I'm like a ghost in the water, paddling, dragging the crate with me. I paddle on
and on. Fatigue spreads through my arms, back, and voice. "I'll get you."
I make it over to Abd al-Wahab, dragging the crate with me. I can feel the exhaustion
in my arms. Abd al-Wahab is close now.
"Give me your hand!" I grab his arm, and something trembles in my chest.

The Argot of Pirates

Collected by Muhammad Lutfi Gumaa, translated by Ben Koerber.

Muhammad Lutfi Gumaa was a prolific Egyptian author who wrote and translated novels (including *Ulysses*), and penned nonfiction on a variety of topics, including folklore, dialect, and Islamic history.

Arabic	Transliteration	Meaning
أويت	ah-WEIT	The sea dog will say to his accomplice, "ma ah-WEIT el-AAMM," meaning "I gave him a bribe"
أشفور	ash-FOOR	A warehouse without any loot
أوه	OO-too	It means "give him a bribe"
أوش أوش	OSH OSH	It means "no no"
أحدى واصل خلوص	AG-dee we IH-mil khal-LOOS	"Beat it, get away from that target"
أون سخي	OWN SAKH-ee	What the sea dogs call a dealer in stolen loot
اشلح العم اللي في خدته	ISH-lah el-AMM ellee fee KHADH-tak	It means "get that third target away"
افتح لاين عشان اشرب من خدته	IF-tah line ashan ish-ta-RATE min KHADH-too	It means "let the target go because I've already robbed him"
برة عنه	barra AAn-noo	It means "get away from him"
بكر	bikr	A warehouse thief
بلال	Bilal	It's the cops!
بابا ديك	ba-ba-DEEK	Grog
بشمو الكبادي جاى	BEET-soo el-ka-BAR-ee GUY	The cops are coming!
تراخي	TRAA-khee	Grub
خينان	khee-tee-YAN	tobacco or smokes
رايق	RIE-ih	A skilled pirate
شهير	shi-HAY-ber	A novice pickpocket
صوان	sa-WANNEE	Gold plunder. A pickpocket will say to his accomplice, "sawani bahu," meaning "barrels of gold"
فيش	feesh	Look!
قدس	qadas	To scram
كسرة	KAS-ra	A piece of wood
مليلة	ma-LEE-la	Soap
الغبر	el-MUH-her	The skilled pirate or looter of ports

مدينة   ma-da-NEE-ya .... A knife or switch-blade
مخزن مربحل   MAKH-zan mer-ING-gil .... A port warehouse full of loot
مخزن شنغيف   MAKH-zan shin-GEEF .... An empty warehouse
مانيلووي   ma-nee-LA-wee .... Type of rope used to tie up a ship
ناحو   NAA-hoo .... Beware! Arrr!
ونت   went .... A treasure chest

The Light Thief

By **Salim A Al-Abbar**

Obsessed with light, the child firmly grasped the portable flashlight when the power failed. Then he went about casting the light all through the house while trying to outrun its beams. He carried the flashlight in his hand as his feet chased the light; he ran everywhere, attempting to catch the cone of brightness that shone in every corner.

In his heedless excitement, he rummaged through things, looking under the beds and in corners we didn't want to be uncovered. We snatched the flashlight from him and shut it off, darkness again engulfing the house. And suddenly, we could no longer hear his voice.

An exhausting search moved through all parts of the house and quickly spread to the dark alleys and dimly lit streets outside. No one could confirm that they had seen him. The neighbors we encountered said only that some kind of light had passed by earlier and then jostled quickly away. The sound that had once pitter-pattered its way across our days and nights had now vanished into an echoing silence that broke only when our minds tricked us into believing he was still there. We were filled with despair. We realized we had lost him forever.

Three months later, when the power went off again, we remembered him. His mother sat alone beside a single candle, her eyes pursuing a butterfly fluttering around the spirals of its flame while two tears, trickling from her broken heart, rolled down her cheeks.

Translated
by Essam M Al-Jassim

Woman

By **Hassan Najmi**

A woman swam in cruelty,
extending her helping arms on the surface of the water.
Saving the sea from certain drowning.

Translated
by Mbarek Sryfi

In the Sea's Playground

By **Ramy al-Asheq**

Translated
by Levi Thompson

I see the sea
as a hole
without a lover's face, reflection,
or waist.
It sucks at the ends, like mud,
like death,
and even those who know the way do not know where it stops.
I see water as a solid
because I am scared of falling, crashing
like a sandcastle fears vanishing, I am scared.
We have met our end more than once,
yet we do not know
who has put off death.
Looking for revenge, I searched for an origin, my origin,
I have never known God so I could thank Him!

Illustration: Dmitri Broido

The Suicides

By **Wadih Saadeh**

Translated
by Suneela Mubayi

Who stormed checkpoints, taboos and fears, who conquered the darkness of the tunnel as they passed through it like a flash of lightning. The suicides – our saints. Who were too large for life, so they made space for themselves in death. Who could not own a life, so they took possession of a death. Who were too sublime for charitable donations, for hospitality that was incidental, for dinner tables where they dish for consumption, so they slammed the door shut behind them and left. Who left the seats and prattle of promises, and went to their silence. Who dissolved the salt of the spirit and pushed it into the waterfall. Who tossed the bread of redemption to the fish. Who silenced the vicious rustling of the brain and became still. There was some mix-up that brought us here, they said, and a mix-up will take us away, so let's just go on our own. Let us be the mix-up ourselves. They left those at work to inherit and be the inheritors, and went to the void. The void that stands high above, above all property or legacy. The void, dark and frightening, which lit up their passing and made friends with it. The void, where the suicides have a spot, a seat they can rest on. Where they have a home, trees and land no one knows. There, they have a rooftop in nothingness where no one but the dead can sit, a tall jasmine tree in front of their home, whose flowers they cannot smell unless they become air. The suicides have sheep that got lost, who they go to tend. There, they celebrate their wedding, without bride or groom, nor any children. They celebrate the impossibility of mating, of the vanishing of their progeny, of the land gone extinct. Every time one of them falls into the water, a new wave is born. Every time one drops into empty space, a fresh breeze blows. The suicides invent new seas and winds. When they dangle from ropes, they fill the empty distance between the ceiling and the floor tiles. They bring something into nothingness.

And when their corpse is carried, the carriers find what they thought was behind them to be walking in front of them. They find the dead corpse ahead of the living body, the past walking after the future and death preceding life. They find that life is in the corpse, not in the body. Only those brimming with life commit suicide. Those so full of it that it spilled over. Only those who rise above death commit suicide. Those who become its masters. Suicides gift meaning to death. They conquer it. Those who commit suicide leave two blots. One on the face of life and another on the face of death. They leave traces of their dominion. And can there be any other dominion? But to be masters is not the suicides' demand. Erasure is their demand. The erasure of the supremacy of life and that of death. The supremacy of those who brought them and of those who take them away. The supremacy of the other and of the self. The erasure that is the supremacy of existence is an act of liberation.

The suicides are our saints, the masters of erasure, masters of the void. And as they relinquish their spirits to the void, they are not relinquishing a life but instead are delivering a condemnation. Instead of relinquishing a corpse, they deliver the name of a killer. Instead of giving up redemption, they hand over particles of dust. When they relinquish their breaths, they relinquish emptiness.

The Government Sea

By **Najwa Binshatwan**

Translated
by Sawad Hussain

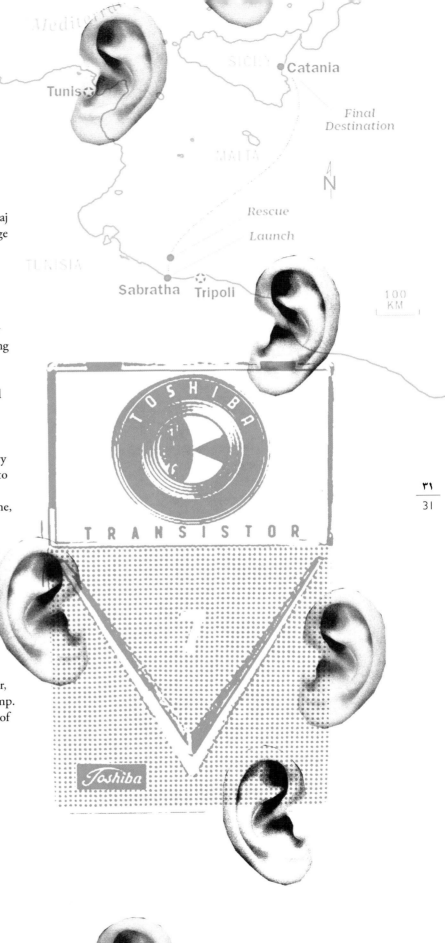

1 "The sea ran away to Malta, *uqsim billah*," Haji Faraj
swore to his fellow patients without pulling the large
Toshiba radio from his ear.

"Maaaaalta?!" the men gathered around him cho-
rused, their mouths one quarter open, one quarter
shut.

Haji Faraj pressed the radio to his ear even harder,
shocked at the sight of the ugly void left behind by
the sea. "Don't look, don't look," he advised. "Seeing
the emptiness will hurt you. The whole scene—it
makes you think of the end times."

"All this ugliness laid bare in front of us today used
to be underwater. God have mercy on us. Who'd
believe that we'd been swimming year after year in
such garbage and lived to tell the tale?"

From sheer dread, one of Haji's friends began to cry
so hard his teeth chattered. "Our s-s-sea ran away to
M-m-alta. What a d-disaster!"

"Why did it decide to up and go now?" another one,
who didn't have any teeth to chatter, asked.

"Maybe it was scared…like us."

"You're thinking of Sha'ban's woman, not the sea."

"Sha'ban? Who's that?"

"Sha'ban—whose wife ran away from him just
like our sea ran away from us."

"Where will it go? Our sea doesn't have any relatives around here except for the Mediterranean
by Malta."

"Malta refused entry to any runaway seas today."

Angered, one of the men stomped against the floor,
making the stale bowl of spaghetti by the door jump.
Cockroaches scurried out to seize the caked dregs of
noodles and sauce that spilled out of the airborne
bowl.

"Who said that?" someone asked as cockroaches
darted over his toes.

"Haji Faraj's radio," said the man whose shirt was
now stained with sauce.

"Now that the sea's run away, what we couldn't see before is now in broad daylight," added another. "Dead fish, migrant bodies, and all sorts of garbage. Before, the surface was swollen with jellyfish, sea turtles, and boats abandoned by those who'd decided to travel by foot instead."

That evening, Haji Faraj's radio – with its contradictory declaration that the sea hadn't run away, but had drowned – stirred up an entirely new commotion.

"Our sea has drowned, everyone. As usual, you don't believe me. I swear to you that it drowned to death and that its body has been disposed of in some far-off place."

"*Really*, Faraj?" someone asked, gripping a piece of bread and a small onion. The rest of them clenched what hair they had left and sank to their knees, weeping.

The night nurse, who was skilled at chopping chicken and onions, chimed in. "Of course it drowned, a painful death. Just look at all the migrant bodies that filled it up, and still there was no drainage system installed. Just look at all that trash and sewage."

"Why didn't *we* die?" the man with breadcrumbs asked.

The funereal scene ended in onion tears.

2 When the central government announced a plan to rebuild what the war had devastated, the municipality put forth a request to establish a sea. Unlike other requests, which usually lingered in a state of neglect, tucked away in drawers, the central government responded right away, as they didn't have any drawers in their offices in which to hide such paperwork.

"We used to go down there every day to swim and have fun, as if we were setting off for work—always at the same time, unless someone had diarrhoea or needed their insulin shot. If someone came to dive, they'd find the whole shore empty because all of us were down in the depths. And if someone came to soak up some sun, they'd see only our heads popping out of the sand, with no space left for theirs. If someone went to have a heart-to-heart with God, he'd find people there before him, doing just that. And if he wanted to spend time alone on the beach, he'd find everyone there already, alone."

Everyone who was using the relatively new sea was of the older generation, since the youth had left for the big cities. It was because of one of these young people, who had left to work in the central government, that the permission to establish a sea in his far-off town was expedited. His father was Haji Faraj himself, carrier of the red radio, who never stopped following and transmitting the news, even when the radio was in Abdullah Nakir's shop for repair.

"You got a smoke?"

"Hardly! No one's come to visit me in a long time."

"Why?"

"Because of the war. Maybe my family's been killed … they might … only God knows," said Sha'ban, the man whose wife had run away.

3 Haji Faraj reached the shore with his radio, where he found his fellow patients trying to read a strange sign, the corners of which were soggy.

A couple of them were patting themselves down for their glasses, while others apologized for not bringing them along in the first place. Several drew near and then retreated from the sign, trying to decipher the mysterious characters inscribed on it. Then the hand of God was with them, as it always is in group activities, and they were able to read the sign at midday:

SEA UNDER MAINTENACE.
NO SWIMMING ALLOWED!

When the old men understood what the sign said,

they rumbled and grumbled and roared, protesting the timing of such maintenance, the decline of government services, and of many other things, such as the Abu al-Walad cheese, as if without a sea they would cease to exist.

Indeed, the following day, that was just what happened: they ceased to exist. Every. Single. One. The sign indicating that the sea wasn't fit for swimming stood atop a pile of rubble and the men's bloody limbs, unaffected by the devastation that had struck. Two years on from their deaths, the government set aside a budget to build a new mental hospital as a replacement for the old one, which had been the site of a different sort of madness.

In an attempt to pacify the souls of the deceased— those for whom the original mental hospital had been opened, and with whom it came to an end—and for the benefit of the new patients who would inaugurate this new hospital, the government decided to situate the hospital somewhere with a real sea view, confirming that they took into consideration the needs of their citizens, both the dead and the living.

Haji Faraj's radio did not communicate this tremendous news. Not because bad news was his speciality, God forbid, but rather because the terrorist bomb that had blown up the hospital left only the laundry room and a few patient wards where several bodies were left whole.

Haji Faraj's corpse was still grasping the radio that had managed to stay in one piece.

His corpse, however, didn't survive falling off the paramedic's stretcher as they transported him to the ambulance: the first time his dentures rolled into the pocket of one of the paramedics, and the second time his nose broke, or maybe it was his collarbone that cracked, but he was truly broken.

It became clear to Haji Faraj's corpse that the stiffness of Sha'ban's legs was preventing him from being put in the ambulance. He might as well make the most of being repeatedly dropped and help mankind somehow. After all, Sha'ban was a kind man. The kind ones were always underappreciated, just as an ambulance is always being used for things other than saving those in need.

As such, and as smoothly as he could, Haji Faraj dropped himself onto Sha'ban's body, cutting off the oxygen tubes and the blood that were being pumped in, putting an end once and for all to his friend's tribulations.

"One madman is the cause of another's killing," the driver of the ambulance muttered to the gravekeeper, who gave a quick glance as he gestured for the burial permit and a cigarette.

Before the flame could touch the cigarette, the ambulance lurched forward, as if it were a donkey trundling along, knowing where to go and how to come back at any time without the slightest hesitation.

Then, with a quiet that the sky of this warring city lacked, the ambulance left the graveyard just as it had entered, a donkey knowing its way.

For those who want to listen to the radio, Haji Faraj lies at rest in plot 40.

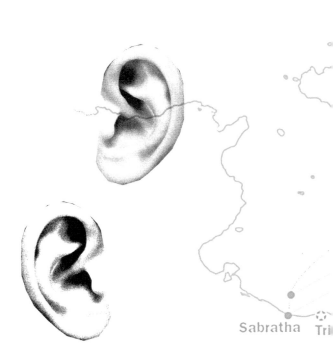

I Bit My Tail, and It Tasted So Good

By **Ahmed Naji**

Translated
by Spencer Scoville

1 I found them at the edge of ISIS's territory after a journey through dozens of neighborhoods and cities. I'd encountered disorganized military camps, pledged allegiance to (and joined) the "governments" of three different "princes," even got married—though the French had bombed our home just two weeks later. I hadn't worried about gathering up her body parts. Martyrs don't require washing, and, in any case, there wouldn't have been anything left to bury. I'd set off on a journey after this voice, as if it were a vision from God. How could I not when the voice had recited His verses?

Then I reached that gray point near the Turkish border. I found their black banner with the single word, "Persevere."

I availed myself of the required generosity by staying three days. On the fourth day, after evening prayers, we walked toward the Tree of Peace. Five elders and two young men sat interrogating me. The Prince, who could not have been more than ten years old, sat silently in the midst of them, his eyes fixed on me. My ears, my heart, all of my senses waited for even the slightest whisper from him, any indication that the voice that I had been following all of these nights was truly his voice. But not a single letter escaped his lips. Sometimes, he would simply nod when I answered a question, as if encouraging me to say more. In the end, he raised his little palm, its fingers clenched except the pinky. An elderly man seated next to him gestured for me to come forward.

I sat at the feet of the brown child prince, and one of the young men on my right read me the text of the pledge, which I repeated: "I bear witness that there is no god but God, and that Muhammad is God's prophet, and that Heaven is real, and that Hell is real, and that our prince, Bakkar of the Small and Delicate Palm, our Prince of the Small and Delicate Palm, is the promised mahdi. I pledge my allegiance to him in victory or martyrdom, and I will not ever betray this promise even if I taste of death. I will de-fend him with my blood, my money, my father, and my mother until the end of time, and we will follow him on the path of those whom God has favored with His grace, not those who are condemned by Him or lost."

Prince Bakkar stretched out his pinky finger, and I extended mine as well. When the two fingers met, I felt that all the chaos of the world had passed away, that my pain had disappeared, and I felt the tears were finally drying on my cheeks.

2 The government had arrested my father and seized our assets and shops. I was in high school when it happened: the event that made me divide my life, for the next seven years, between begging from my uncles and chasing after government employees, begging them to raise the amount that they'd pay from our frozen assets. And, of course, visiting my father in prison, where he died.

I got a job as a doctor in the camp for illegal immigrants in al-Alamein. It was not my role to care for immigrants, of course, but to care for their body parts, which were exported to Europe. After signing the cultural privacy agreement for Mediterranean countries, an electrified steel fence was erected that divided the North from the South, and the European governments increased their financial contributions to the Arab generals and the weapons that they exported and donated to them, in exchange for their promise to take the role of supervising the prisoners. Detention camps for the illegal immigrants were established all along the southern coast of the Mediterranean. Civil society organizations rose up, together with the Green and European Left parties to support these poor immigrants through various development programs. One was the project that I work in, that of trading body parts for "local opportunities."

Imagine yourself a poor young man who wants to travel to Europe. You are arrested and placed in a prison camp. Analysts and sociological specialists undertake a study of your condition, and they re-plan your future. They tell you, "You have wonderful skills. You're good at cooking, so we would like to offer you a deal you can't refuse—you can donate a kidney or a piece of your liver to this poor Swiss child so he can live and make his family happy, and, in exchange, we will provide you with a cart from which you can sell liver and sausage sandwiches." Of course, after a month of happily standing in front of the liver cart, in this situation that has been brought about through the slavery of your employment, the police come to cite your cart for violating regulations: you have utilized a deep-fat fryer in a public space in violation of the Paris Accords on Climate Change and Global Warming, and the cycle of your unhappiness begins again. You start from a beginning that seems exactly like the end, just like someone who bites his own tail, who pays for his misfortune from his own hide.

I became friends with many of the foreigners and European girls who came to help the refugees and immigrants by teaching them to draw or play classical music, or other queer activities for which white European culture is famous. I took advantage of every opportunity that presented itself to insert my cock into that white Mediterranean flesh on the chance that one of them would be driven crazy enough to marry me and take me with her, but my white knight never appeared, so I tried to make a life by selling the organs that were rotting in the local freezers of the organ-harvesting hospitals in Egypt.

3 I didn't hear the sound of a bullet the whole time I stayed in Prince Bakkar's state, as if we were in a paradise hidden from the rockets and the military units and the brigades on the prowl. A quiet life of worshipping and remembering God. I noticed that the military drills weren't serious, and that the focus was on spiritual development. One day, the police commander asked me to hand over all my weapons, allowing me to keep just one revolver.

The mountains were green here in our land, and pure water flowed down in little falls, forming pools and small lakes around which we'd often spend our nights chanting and worshipping until dawn prayer and the rising of the sun. While we were returning from the lake to the land of our state one evening, Brother 'Abd al-Rahman revealed to me, after a lengthy religious introduction, that he loved me in God, trusted my morals, and wanted to give me a gift. He said that he found no better gift than his sister's hand in marriage. Brother 'Abd al-Rahman was one of the country's native inhabitants, not an immigrant like me, so his offer was a huge honor, and I saw love in his eye: the bond of pure brotherhood, the sure connection that does not come undone, the rope of God to which we hold fast, persevering.

4 One of the detainees had approached me, once, in the illegal immigration camp. We exchanged greetings, dope, and pills. He informed me that he had a connection in an Italian hospital who could smuggle him to Europe with my help—me, a young doctor who had not yet earned his Master's.

"Me? How? If I knew, I would've gotten myself out of this rotting swamp."

He said his connection would send a request for some organs with certain characteristics, all of which would line up with his. Then my part would begin—I was to dissect him, cutting him to pieces, placing his body in freezers and storage containers. Since the first rule of the Mediterranean Commercial Agreement was, "Yes to the freedom of movement for goods, no to the freedom of movement for people," his body would be transported as a commodity to where his "connection" in Italy could gather up the parts and bring him back to life.

"That's impossible—it can't happen. Life is God's business. Your connection can't bring you back if I cut up your body," I told him. "That's a risk I will not take."

He got angry and told me it was too late, and that he would carry out his plan whether I agreed or not. A few days later, I received a report from the Italian hospital he'd mentioned, and I began preparing and gathering the requested materials, some of which had to be taken fresh from living bodies.

A few weeks later, I learned that they had come across a corpse in a structure near the camp that had been used as a secret abortion clinic for the migrants who were raped by the peace-keeping and Mediterranean troops. His corpse was sliced down the middle, devoid of any internal organs.

Then they ended the program. The European Union announced new measures. They made clear that artificial organs were more economical than biological ones, which had to be harvested and imported, and that consequently there was no longer any need to continue the program, "Organs and Local Opportunities." I was kicked out of the camp, and the door closed on opportunities to travel. I returned again to the swamp, with neither hope nor despair.

5

I spent two years of my life among the mujahidin here. Every day, before falling asleep, I would pray to God that He would grant me His blessing in the form of martyrdom. When I reached the land of the little Prince and joined the forces of Prince Bakkar Of the Small and Delicate Palm, I prayed to God that He grant me heaven and the next life in the company of His prophet and my prince.

I married 'Abd al-Rahman's sister. He was a true brother, and his sister was a faithful, obedient, fruitful wife—clean of body and home. She was ready to give birth to our first child any day.

News and rumors spread through the community, and after prayers on Friday, the Prince of the Small Palm ascended the minbar and sat. He praised God, pronounced *bismillah*, and in a beautiful voice began to recite from Sura al-Anfal. Tears poured down our faces as his voice poured the precious word of

God into our hearts, purifying us. Prince Bakkar's voice was the surest evidence that he was indeed the long-awaited *mahdi*. Our hearts rested in his voice, and the revealed word of God was manifest in his recitation, clear and wonderful in its miraculous power. When he finished, our eyes were focused and our bodies receptive to what he would say. Instead, he gestured to one of his counselors, who climbed the minbar and gave a sermon that confirmed the spreading rumors.

After the second defeat at Mosul and the withdrawal of the brothers of the Islamic State, as well as those who had pledged allegiance to the Caliph al-Baghdadi, the siege of all the provinces in the state intensified— even those that had not been sucked into the previous Iraqi morass. The Europeans had achieved a ceasefire with the provinces that were not fighting in Mosul or Iraq, including our own. The Sheikh announced that the Prince had received a delegation from the French army, which was attempting to mediate between the provinces allied with the Islamic State and the Russians. The negotiations had not reached any definite conclusion. Then the Sheikh said, by way of concluding his remarks and quoting from Sura al-Anfal, "And if they incline to peace." Before the murmurings and protests could rise, the voice of the little Prince rose up, completing the Qur'anic recitation, and the group fell silent. A white dove entered the mosque, rose high, and alighted on his shoulder. Hearts softened and eyes fixed on the miracle of the white dove which, after a moment, rose up suddenly. All of those present followed the path of its flight.

6

I returned again to live at home with my mother after I was fired at the camp. Every day, I stopped in at the private hospitals, looking for temporary work, or for a single day on call. I had no fixed source of income, no money to finish my studies and get my Master's degree, no fellowship to change from being a general practitioner to a specialist.

My uncle came and visited us, and he mentioned a friend of his who worked in Iraq. They were looking for young doctors to work for salaries between three and five thousand dollars a month.

"Sign me up, uncle," I said.

The work was technically on Iraqi soil, but not inside Iraq. My mother borrowed money from her brother. I tried to travel to Turkey, but I was stopped at the airport, prohibited from traveling for security reasons—or, more accurately, because of my father's security and political files. My uncle said this would force me to take the overland route, which is cheaper and more profitable. I traveled by bus to the southern end of Sinai, then covertly from Nuweiba to the port of Aqaba in Jordan, then into the camps in Jordan, and from there to the borders of the Islamic State in Iraq and Syria.

I worked at first as a mujahid doctor in Adnani's brigade. We had a small hospital on the back lines, where the work was like in any Egyptian hospital. Then I heard, for the first time, about the brigades of the Boy Prince. They did not kill Shiites, yet all the other brigades feared and respected them. They were completely autonomous in their province. Even though they paid taxes to the State, they did not request its weapons or support, and they were committed to providing aid whenever it was asked of them. They all obeyed the Boy Prince with the magical voice before whose charm and sweetness you could do nothing but smile and comply.

I believed this story was just a local fable up until I first married. From the day we struggled and slept next to each other for the first time, my wife informed me that she hoped to travel to the province of Prince Bakkar, and that this was the only place to raise a child.

"But is that group even real?" I asked her. "Besides—I heard that they're on the northern border along the front lines, being bombed by the Russians and Turks. How can they be in that place?"

She took out the iPad I had given her as a dowry, then connected it to the speakers. The voice of the young boy Bakkar poured out of them. A bullet of light pierced my ear and blew my mind. The world was no longer as it had been. The grey "filter" that had colored everything around me fell away. "*We returned your sight to you, and your sight this day is sharp.*" When my wife was martyred in the French bomb attack, I set off, searching for the voice of the little prince.

7

On the day my wife gave birth to the child we named Qasim, everyone in the community was called to gather at the mosque.

The little prince ascended. This time, he spoke alone, and he did not stop at reciting from the Qur'an.

The Prince said that the sanctity and preservation of Muslim blood stood above all other considerations. He followed these statements with other, similar ideas, and, in the end, things were as follows: According to an agreement with the Russians, as the other party in the agreement, and with the French and the Europeans, who were witnesses and mediators, all who pledged allegiance to Prince Bakkar were granted complete immunity for any crimes they had committed, and it was illegal for any security forces in Syria to prosecute them for any reason. In exchange, the tribe must turn over all its weapons and move to the closest city, leaving the mountains and the grasslands behind, which was exactly what we did. The last point required a great deal of discussion and consideration, resulting in the prince and his tribe explaining that our pledge to the prince had not passed away, but that we would continue to observe all of our rites—even increase our observance of them—so that the ties between us would strengthen, as a group capable of continued growth and development, not like a group of mercenaries brought together by war to plunder and profit.

When Qasim turned one, I was appointed a deputy in the city's Department of Health. I am now a citizen of Syria. I have submitted to the Assad regime, and in exchange they granted us the right to direct the affairs of the city in accordance with Islamic law, through a police force controlled by some of our brothers from the "Persevere" group.

We have been saved from defeat and slaughter, and we have traded the forest and countryside villages for ruined cities that we quickly began to rebuild and restore with funds from the West and those Arabs that follow them. A picture of Assad hangs high on every rebuilt building, but next to it hangs a picture of our little Prince Bakkar. Some idiots think that he is Assad's son, but even they recognize the power of our organization over this city that has fallen entirely under our control, as if we were an independent province functioning within a federal government.

One day, I went to work to find a delegation from the European Union on a humanitarian mission, as usual, with a new project: selling used prosthetics and artificial organs to citizens and victims through an EU-funded program. These humanitarian organizations would buy the artificial kidneys, for example, from the family of a poor Swiss child, take care of them, and then sell them to sick Syrians in need. I tried to explain to the prince that they were liars and cheats capable of turning any crime into a humanitarian deed and then selling it to us, though not without ulterior motives. He shook his head and told me, Smile in their faces. You don't have to do anything they ask. Confirm their prejudices of how savage and irretrievably failed we are, and they will quickly give up and leave, only to have another come in their place, selling more weapons and presenting more charitable donations.

Qasim was asleep in my arms, and I was thinking about this cycle that endlessly repeats, and about my own destiny—how I started with the desire to travel to Europe and work there, and how I became a lowly employee in a bureaucratic institution within the Assad government. Good and Evil are two dogs chasing one another's tails. I've bit my own tail—chewed on it, even. It tastes so good.

Our power lies in our prince. In the magic of his voice, which makes everyone obey and believe in his blessings and miracles. They invited me to his noble palace high on the mountain. I entered the room, and at a gesture from his hand everyone else was asked to leave. When they left, he greeted me, saying: "*As-Salaam 'alaykum*, my good doctor."

In that instant, I understood the problem, and I knew the disaster that had beset us.

The entire organization fell apart in just a couple of weeks. When they pressed the sheikhs and the counselors to find a solution to the problem, I told them the time had passed. It would have been possible to do something before he reached puberty, to preserve his vocal cords, but now the signs of puberty had already appeared, or, as I put it, he'd already had his first wet dream. There was no way to repair things. Our dearly beloved Prince Bakkar of the Delicate Palm had lost his voice; it had become something else—rough, manly, with no sweetness or charm to it at all.

One of Assad's generals came to my office in the hospital. His offer was straightforward and clear: the prince and the "Persevere" group were finished and would soon be broken up. There was no longer anyone to protect me. I could either return to Egypt, where they would review my file and have their way with me, or I would transfer to work as a doctor in the Syrian army, based on my experience, where I could hold any number of positions. I requested some time to consider the matter, but he said: "Only until tomorrow, Doctor. In the morning, a green car will come to the hospital to take you. You'll be the one who tells the driver if you want to head to the airport, and from there to Cairo, or if you want to give yourself over to the protection of the armed forces of the great Syrian Arab Army."

Nobody Mourns the City's Cats

By **Muhammad El-Hajj**

Illustrations: Hassān Al Mohtasib, modeled after Tinatin Meparishvili

Translated by
Yasmine Zohdi

As soon as I
settled into the
kitchen chair,
she jumped on my
lap.

"The little
bitch!
She never does
that with me!"

Mistika was a mountain cat Fatma had found a few months back while taking a stroll on a beach in Sinai. A few bedouin children had been throwing around a tiny ball of fur, and it wasn't until Fatma heard the soft, hoarse meows that she realized they were playing with an actual newborn kitten. She screamed at them and they ran, leaving the kitten on the sand in a state of near-collapse. The next day, Fatma brought her along to Cairo, checking her into a vet's clinic for a few days before taking her home to the apartment. For weeks, she filled Facebook with pictures of Mistika, trying to find someone to adopt her, but the cat's wild nature remained an obstacle. She'd been with Fatma for six months, hiding in obscure corners throughout the day, scratching Fatma's hand whenever she tried to touch her, avoiding guests and eating only when Fatma went out and the apartment was empty. Only when Fatma turned on the heater during cold days would Mistika come out to sleep underneath it.

Now she was on my lap, and I stroked her head as Fatma looked on, amused.

"Perhaps you should take her, Hazem. She might bring you some comfort," she said.

Her suggestion made me uneasy. I continued to stroke Mistika's back, and her body relaxed for a minute before she hissed and scratched my hand. I got up, annoyed, and she dropped off my lap and quickly ran inside. Fatma laughed. "I was wrong. It seems not even the cat wants you."

The doorbell rang. Fatma stepped away from the counter where she'd been mixing the batter for her pancakes and gestured for me to stay put. She headed out to open the door, and I heard the doorman ask for her share of the fees to fix the elevator. She told him she'd speak to the landlord about it and closed the door.

"Did he see you come up earlier?" she asked nervously.

"No, he didn't."

"I don't understand. My landlord just talked to me about this yesterday. Something's not right."

I didn't give much weight to her anxiety. Fatma had recently moved out of her parents' house after years of arguing about it. She'd tried to persuade them at times, angrily lashed out at others, and would sometimes leave to stay with her grandmother for weeks or months on end. It was almost like a traditional prison-break story, where one tests the limits of their guards' capabilities before setting out on a long, elaborate plan for escape, and where — in addition to the pain of confinement — they also have to deal with the fear of being caught. Years of living with a father intent on exercising his authority over everyone under his roof and a mother who'd lost the ability to live outside such a toxic environment had saddled Fatma with an intuitive skepticism toward the world. This was why I'd learned to ignore most of her worries, particularly those having to do with why the waiter gave her that look or why my girlfriend hated her or why whomever wouldn't call her back. Fatma was trying to make out some voices coming from the alley beneath the kitchen window as I opened the fridge, took out a green apple, washed it, then went back to my chair and started to eat. The crunching sound brought her attention back to me. "You'll ruin your appetite! Who am I making these pancakes for?"

I didn't care about the pancakes. I could feel my indignation at her earlier comment about the cat rise again within me. I left the half-eaten apple on the counter. "I'm going out for a smoke."

From the balcony, I gazed out at Abdeen Palace. It had always stirred my curiosity. Many times, I'd imagined myself as a 19th-century textile merchant from al-Azhar who knew nothing of the world beyond the alleyways of al-Sayeda, the nooks and crannies of the neighborhoods around the Citadel, and the trip from the shrine of al-Hussein to that of Fatima. How strange it would have felt for me, then, to suddenly come across this neoclassical structure — to see it there, looming before me, irrevocably changing the route I'd taken for years? To find myself standing before it — in the heart of my own city, in the heart of all that's dear and familiar — and feeling small, excruciatingly small?

Oh well. Extravagance always made me think of nothingness. More attempts at distraction, all to no avail. Khedive Ismail ended up in debt and exile, and my relationship with Aya had come to a similar fate.

"I'm sorry," Fatma's voice came from behind me.

She stepped closer, leaning against the railing as she looked at me. I smiled, and she gently touched my cheek. We'd been playing the same role in turns throughout the ten years we'd been friends; she'd take care of me, and then I'd take care of her, and sometimes we'd both be in so much pain that neither of us could hear the other. Yet the comfort of knowing we were not alone was always enough to make it better.

Fatma took me by the hand and walked me back to the kitchen. She'd finished the batter and started to pour it into the pan. She talked about a bunch of things all at once, and I knew she was intentionally blocking every opening in the conversation where a certain subject could be brought up. I didn't mind. I wasn't going to ask her anyway—not directly at least. I knew no good would come of trying to find out what she was hiding. But I grew bored when she talked about Bassem's birthday party without mentioning she'd met Aya there.

"Fatma, why are you doing this?"

"Doing what?"

"You're teasing. I know everything already, so why do you keep going around in circles?"

"You know Aya's seeing someone?"

What a fool I was. I wished I hadn't spoken. Of course I hadn't known, but I should've. Damn it, Aya. A new relationship? Already? It had been only six weeks since our stormy breakup. Was that how it goes? She'd called me a couple of weeks ago, and I'd been eager to answer, but something had held me back from picking up the first time. But there hadn't been a second, and I spent days fighting the urge to call her back to find out what she'd wanted to tell me. Had she wanted me back? Had she finally come to realize I was the only man for her? By the end of the week, I'd convinced myself that her kitchen sink was probably blocked, and she'd only called to ask me for the plumber's number upon discovering she didn't have it. Now I knew she only wanted to do the decent thing and be the one to tell me she was seeing someone new, and when I never called her back, she simply let herself off the hook.

"She's seeing someone?"

"Yeah. She brought him to the party."

"Who is he?"

"I don't know, I'd never met him before.
Do you know Hadeer?"

"Hadeer Sebaei?"

"Yes."

"Not personally."

"He's her ex."

I could feel a wave of melancholy slowly wash over me. Our relationship had died months before we'd actually ended it, like a cold body lying dead in the bedroom that we wouldn't talk about but couldn't really ignore, either. I'd told myself it would subside after a while, that perhaps if I waited — a week, two weeks, a month, ten years — I'd be rewarded for my patience. But Aya was firmer than that. She'd hesitated for months, out of fear of what her life would look like after the end, but she eventually decided: there were no more paths left for us to tread together, because our destinations weren't the same. Despite my pain, I couldn't help but admire her resolve. She knew what she wanted, and I wasn't it.

"What's he like?"

"Well, he looks like you, sort of. Tall and skinny."

My head teemed with questions. How did they act together? Did she touch him, or did she worry people would tell me what they saw? Was he better-looking than me? Funnier, maybe? Was he elegant or disheveled? I ordered myself to stop. There was no use talking or thinking about it. The pancakes were ready. I helped Fatma take the plates out of the cupboard and carry them out to the dining table.

We sat down to eat. The day wasn't going the way I'd imagined. Fatma had been knee-deep in preparing for her PhD exams when she noticed that it had been a while since we'd last met, so she'd called me to join her for breakfast on her day off. I'd thought that, to make it up to me, she would shower me with food and affection and lovingly listen to me as I ranted about everything. None of that was happening. She was constantly glancing at the clock to make sure the free time she'd allowed herself for the day hadn't yet ended, and I was consumed with thoughts of Aya and her new boyfriend. Halfway through our pancakes, we heard the jingle of keys outside the door. Fatma tensed, but seconds later her roommate Alia walked in, followed by Hassan, an actor I'd met a few times. He'd starred in numerous independent theater productions before recently landing a big role in a film. Alia

started when she saw us at the table. For a brief moment she looked disappointed, but then she smiled as she took off her shoes by the door.

"Simsim, you're here! I thought you were teaching today."

"I didn't go, habibti," Fatma told her. "Join us, I made pancakes."

"We've got some work to do, but we'll come out in a bit—"

"Nope! I want to eat now," Hassan interrupted. He bent down to hug Fatma before taking a seat at the table while Alia glared at him. At that moment, Mistika walked out, scanning the room with her eyes. She steadily made her way toward me before jumping onto my lap once more. Alia watched, astonished.

"Simsim! Did you see what that bitch just did?" Alia exclaimed.

Fatma looked at me with a grin. "What did I say?"

"She hates everyone! How did you get her to like you?"

I was busy chewing on pancakes and strawberries, so I didn't answer, but it appeared that Mistika had managed to break the ice. A lively conversation ensued; Hassan told us how the vet tried to steal his wife's cat and claimed she'd run away, while Alia spoke of the beloved cat she'd left at her mother's house. The afternoon sunlight flitted in through the old curtains, bathing our faces, and the smoke from the joint Hassan lit after we'd finished eating swirled over our heads.

But the peace was only fleeting. Fatma's phone rang. It was her brother, Ahmad, a correspondent for the New York Times. She canceled the call, but he called Alia. Fatma sighed and took the call to the balcony. She returned a few minutes later.

"It looks like there's another raid today."

Alia looked alarmed, while Hassan continued to grind the hashish, unperturbed.

It had all started a few days ago with a tweet warning downtown residents that the police would be searching apartments and making arrests ahead of the impending anniversary of the 18-day uprising. Nobody knew the person who sent the tweet, so it didn't get much attention. But the raid did happen, wildly escalating over two days. In a phone interview on a TV talk show, the deputy to the Minister of Interior boasted that the police had broken into nearly five thousand rentals in and around downtown. It was a well-known routine: The informers would turn the apartment upside down, terrorizing the residents, holding on to whatever "evidence" they came across (old protest flyers, for instance, or books about human rights), before inspecting their email and Facebook accounts. The officer would begin by scrolling through your profile, and if they found any posts against the ruling regime... let's say it wouldn't turn out well. One activist had a post advising comrades to keep a piece of hashish at hand, just in case: offer it to the officer and he might refrain from going through your social media and take you in for drug use instead — a much simpler charge.

"Calm down, Fatma. We're far from Qasr al-Aini," I said.

"Ahmad just hung up. He says they have information from sources within the MoI."

"Well, let's wait until we know what's happening. There's no need to panic now."

Fatma turned to Hassan, still busy with the hashish. He looked up at her, and his nonchalance seemed to calm her. "Good that you have some hash. We might need it."

Hassan cleaned off his hands and reached up, bringing Fatma to sit down next to him. He kissed the top of her head, handed her the remaining piece of hashish, then looked at me and gestured toward the door. I knew we couldn't stay; the presence of two men who weren't relatives would make matters much worse for Fatma and Alia.

I was putting on my coat and scarf in the kitchen when I heard Fatma call me. I walked out, and she asked me to follow her into her room.

"Listen, I've had these euros ever since I was in Berlin, and this hard drive has all my thesis research. I can't risk anything happening to them," she said. "Keep them with you, I'll take them back when this is over."

I placed the money and the hard drive in the inside pockets of my coat. Then she hugged me so tight I no longer found it in me to be mad at her. I gave her a light kiss on the cheek before turning to head out of the room, and she playfully punched my shoulder. I turned back around, puzzled.

"You didn't hug me back properly," she said.

"Well, you pissed me off, Fatma. You really did."

"And that's why I was hugging you. I'm trying to say sorry, again!"

"I'll hug you better next time."

She laughed and threw a book from the pile on her desk at me, I ducked and chuckled before running out to catch Hassan at the door.

Downstairs, in the entryway to the building, the doorman stood with a man who looked unmistakably like a policeman in civilian clothing. I whispered my suspicions to Hassan, but he dismissed the idea. Then we walked past them.

"Were you upstairs, gentlemen?"

"Yes, we were."

"Who were you visiting?"

It was ridiculous. The doorman interrogating us with the support of a police informer. I was this close to swearing at him when Hassan spoke: "At the dentist's."

"On the second floor?"

"You're the doorman, and you're asking me what floor the dentist is on?"

Normally, Hassan's reply would have resulted in an obnoxious response, and probably more obnoxious questions. Perhaps they would have asked for our IDs, perhaps worse. One night, a friend of mine was driving a mutual friend of ours — a woman — home from a party in Maadi, when an officer stopped them, asking for his driving license, and demanding to know their relationship. When my friend answered, he sounded bored, which the officer didn't like. He ordered him to pull over, which my friend did. Then he put our mutual friend in a taxi and went back to the officer, asking — a little sharply — why he was being kept. My friend ended up being beaten to a pulp at the police station, after being accused of assaulting an officer on duty. At that point, the best we could do was frantically search for any acquaintances within the ministry who could help us persuade the officer to drop the charges. Such stories were pretty standard; they evoked no surprise and no sorrow. Such was life in Cairo: a gamble and a constant test of shrewdness, good sense, and self-control. That was why Egyptians always sang about the cruelty of life, and about time as the ultimate teacher. It was brutal, yes, but it also forced you

"Hey, asshole. I'm talking to you."

to be aware of the fragility of the world —valuable wisdom that was usually hard to grasp.

Hassan took a risk by responding sarcastically, but his bet was well-placed. He bet on our appearances: our wool coats, our leather shoes, my stylish eyeglasses, and his shiny Swiss watch. The informer kept the doorman from asking any more questions and signaled us to pass.

We finally walked out onto the street. I patted my inside pockets, making sure Fatma's hard drive and money were safe inside, while Hassan lit a cigarette. We walked across downtown, surrounded by a seemingly endless stream of police cars on their way to break into the private spaces of other people, the most unfortunate of which we would hear about the next day, when news about those who'd been detained reached us in the form of Facebook posts.

I didn't really have anywhere to go. My apartment had been cold ever since Aya left, my mother was in Alexandria preparing for her retirement, my sister was in the States with her husband and their daughter. I thought of someone else I could see, but quickly scratched the idea. Hassan interrupted my chain of thoughts by asking if I wanted to play a round of backgammon at the ahwa. I shrugged, and we made our way back towards Strand. Amr was on shift — he was downtown's most elegant head waiter, with his crisp white shirt and swift, graceful movements. He nodded when he saw me, the friendliest gesture he'd shown me ever since I started frequenting Strand ten years ago, but his expression changed as soon as he noticed Hassan behind me. I ordered a shisha and a cold sobia despite the chilly weather, and Hassan ordered a coffee. By the time Amr returned with our drinks, a police car had stopped on the other side of the street, and a force was descending to make its way into the adjacent building.

"What's happening, Amr?"

"Downtown is on fire, pasha. It's been like this for three days now. Yesterday they came and went and came and went. Then they camped out at the ahwa for four full hours, drank their fill, and left without paying for anything."

"Alright. Bring us a backgammon board."

I glanced at Hassan before we both silently started sipping on our drinks, trying to ignore what we'd just heard, until Amr

came back with the backgammon. For years I'd tried and failed to memorize the Persian names for dice that ahwa-goers in Cairo used with such ease, a fact Hassan didn't fail to remark on. He made another comment about me being a beginner, right before he dealt the final, humiliating blow that ended the round. He almost closed the wooden board — there was no fun in beating beginners, after all — but I insisted we go for a second round. As we played, he kept directing me to the triangles where I should move my pieces, but I refused his advice, because it came from a condescending place, and anyway I didn't want a victory that wasn't earned. I almost got him that time, but he won again. My phone rang as soon as we were done. I looked at the screen and got up to take the call outside. Hassan reached out to close the board, but I signaled him not to, and made my way out.

"Hello."

"Why haven't you been calling me?"

It was complicated. Incredibly complicated, actually.

Dalal and I had met at the movies. I'd been watching a really bad Kurdish film and decided to leave halfway through. She followed me out and told me I'd forgotten my backpack. I took it and thanked her, but she didn't go back inside. She ordered a coke and stood drinking it at the cafeteria. I approached her, saying I had a feeling I'd seen her before, and she reminded me that she'd been to mine and Aya's place, once, when we'd hosted a mutual friend's birthday party. I was surprised — I wouldn't have thought I'd forget a face as beautiful as hers. She said she'd heard me curse the director under my breath in the theater, and I laughed and apologized if I'd ruined the film for her. "Oh, no," she said. "It's a shit film." In a few minutes Aya had returned from the bathroom. She nonchalantly greeted Dalal, then we were on our way. Weeks later, I ran into Dalal again at a bookstore in Zamalek. She told me her grandmother had just died, and I talked of my fear of death--particularly the thought of my mother dying--and my eyes had watered. She suddenly asked if I liked carrot cake; I said I did. She ordered us a slice from the bookstore's cafe, took a bite then almost instantly spit it out onto her plate: "This sucks," she said, and we left. At home, I told Aya about our encounter. She raised her eyebrows without a word. That's when I thought perhaps it would be wiser not to run into Dalal again.

We did run into each other once more, however. That time, Aya and I were going through a rough patch; I'd left our apartment and was staying at a friend's place. We hadn't met for ten days, but the wedding of two of our closest friends forced us to appear together in public. Aya was already there when I arrived. I kissed her, and she left me and headed for the dancefloor. I scanned the room for the bar, only to see Dalal standing there. The coincidences that had brought us together before had stopped once Aya had raised her eyebrows, but some plan beyond my control had led to that moment: me watching Dalal lean against the bar in a sleek black dress that emphasized her beautiful body. I was surprised — I wouldn't have thought I'd forget such full, smooth thighs. I walked toward her and hugged her as though we were good old friends. She seemed as happy to see me as I was to see her. She chided me that we hadn't met for months, I chided her that we hadn't met for months, and we agreed to meet for breakfast two days later. That morning Aya left me, and Dalal and I spent seven hours together.

"Hey, asshole. I'm talking to you."

"I'm here."

"Why haven't you been calling me?"

"Well, we're talking now, aren't we?"

"Are you serious?"

Dalal had that authoritative tone sometimes, and I liked it. I liked the idea of a woman wanting to possess me, much the same way she liked it when I called her after we'd parted at night, to make sure she got home safe.

"Alright, I'm sorry."

"Well, I'll consider your apology. I'll let you know later if it's been accepted."

My relationship with Dalal was evolving in different directions. When I met her the day Aya and I broke up, I'd been planning to spend two, three hours with her, talking about nothing of consequence, before I took a train and went back to Alexandria for a while. What happened, however, was that I spent the entire day with her, moving from one spot to another on Road 9, from morning coffee to lunch to shisha at sunset. I cried, I made jokes, I felt my existence weighing on my chest, I felt

as light as a helium balloon, and I told her everything about everything, as though I'd known her ever since I was a fetus, as though we were strangers who'd just met on a train.

In the weeks that followed, we spoke every single day, for hours sometimes if we didn't meet, but we always met. I'd left my friend's place in Maadi and, after Aya decided to move out, I'd gone back to the apartment I had shared with her. It wasn't always comfortable being there, but facing the ghosts of your past can be a useful exercise, sometimes. I would take Dalal on nightly excursions across the neighborhood: we'd start south, near the Orman Gardens, and walk to its northernmost parameters — the end of Al-Batal Street, where there was a Baskin Robbins. We'd grab some honey chipotle chicken from Chili's on our way, then head to the waffle place in front of the Czech Embassy. We'd pass by the edges of Dayer al-Nahya, dismissing the hostile looks we got from the boys and men lurking on street corners. I would walk, and I would watch Dalal walk — that walk that looked as though she'd just invented it, as though she'd whipped together a collection of movements by different creatures. How does a cat walk? Or a fox? Or a mare? More seriously: How does beauty walk? How does radiance? I was delving into something I couldn't quite fathom with every step we took together.

"Where are you?"

"Downtown."

"Doing what?"

"Nothing."

"I'm at Soha's, come pick me up then."

She was firm. It was the kind of firmness a person was capable of only when they knew just how powerful they were. I considered letting her down, but I really wanted to see her. I imagined she knew what Fatma had told me about Aya, and that was why she'd called me. It was as comforting as it was unsettling. It was heart-warming that she was trying to take care of me, but I felt a twinge of anger stir within me. I didn't want her pity. But God, I missed her. I hadn't spoken to her in two days. I'd dropped by her work earlier in the week when a friend of mine who worked at the same place winked and said it was weird that Dalal saw more of me than he did. I got defensive, but his remark made me uneasy, and when Dalal approached

"I'm here."

I'd grown a little sullen. She asked me what was wrong, I told her, and she called him names and said he was just jealous because he'd asked her out a couple of months back and she hadn't shown much interest. Her response filled me with even more questions, but I didn't voice any of them. I left early that day, and I hadn't spoken to her since.

"Okay. I'll pick you up."

"What time?"

"I'll call you when I'm downstairs."

I went back into the ahwa. Hassan had closed the backgammon board, and I was about to reopen it when he said he wasn't in the mood to play. While I was on the phone, the police had come down with someone he knew from the building across the street, a drummer in an up-and-coming indie band. I asked if he wanted to leave, and he said yes. He got up and headed outside to make some calls — friends, human rights lawyers, and journalists, I guessed. The same old, boring routine. I paid for our order and left the ahwa. Hassan was still on the phone, and he asked where I was going. "Mounira," I replied softly, and he said he'd join me. I wanted to object, but he'd already shifted his focus back to the call. Oh well, why not? I walked, and he followed.

The trip from downtown to Mounira used to be easy; we'd just walk down one long, straight street, starting at Hati al-Geish all the way to Mobtadayan, taking no turns all the way. It was in that street where I stood, one hot August day in 2008, watching the flames and the smoke rise from the parliament building, and thinking about the death of Cairo. What did it take for an old, battered city to fall and rise no more? Perhaps that was the problem; Cairo was far too restless, each time she started to surrender, her imagination prompted her to act, feverishly. Oh, how she promised, and how she betrayed. We were making our way down Mohamed Mahmoud Street now. Police presence was even heavier there, and I bitterly remembered those who'd been killed beneath the walls, on the sidewalks, on the rooftops of the surrounding buildings. Were we more stubborn, or was the dream?

When Soha's building appeared in the distance I brought out my phone to call Dalal. It had died. I held it like a dead fish, not knowing what to do with it, before putting it back in

my pocket. I squeezed my brain, trying to remember Soha's apartment number, but my attempts were cut short when I saw a lock on the gate. I turned to Hassan, who was still on the phone. I signaled him to be quick, and he hung up a few seconds later. I asked if he had Dalal's number, and he said he did. He scrolled through his phone for a moment, then said he didn't after all. I gazed up at Soha's balcony, willing her to look out. I tried to open the gate, although I knew it wouldn't budge. I asked Hassan if he had Foad's number, a mutual friend. He searched until he found it and called him. He was on the phone for three minutes before he came back saying Foad had lost his phone and still hadn't restored most of his contacts on the new one. I looked at the gate again, helplessly. I was about to turn around and leave, but Hassan stopped me saying, he would make one last try. He dialed and waited.

"Sheero! How have you been?" Then: "Are you alright? What's wrong?"

He gave me a concerned look as he spoke. I told him to ask her for the number and get on with it, he signaled me to be patient. It seemed I had to wait until Shereen was done complaining. I was leaning against a tree by the building, waiting for Hassan to finish, when I heard the gate squeak. It was Dalal.

It wasn't the first time I'd seen Dalal appear somewhere — approach from a distance, come out a door or descend a flight of stairs — but a strange comfort grazed my heart at the sight of her. My smile widened as she hugged me. I went on holding her until she comfortingly patted my shoulder and let go. She turned and said hello to Hassan before coming back to stand next to me.

"What took you so long?"

"I came right after we hung up, but the gate was closed, and my phone died, and Hassan couldn't find your number, and Foad lost his phone so Hassan called Shereen to ask her for it but here you are."

"Oh, is that Shereen he's talking to?" She was already moving towards Hassan, asking him to hand her the phone. He gave it to her and asked me for a cigarette. I gave him one before I lit one for myself, while Dalal continued talking to Shereen. She moved closer to me, took the cigarette from my hand, and inhaled as she held my gaze. Then she returned it and continued

"What time?"

pacing and talking. I was a little disconcerted. I looked at Hassan out of the corner of my eye and glimpsed a subtle smile playing on his lips.

"Give me a second, I'll ask them," Dalal was saying.

She asked if we wanted to go over to Shereen's. Hassan instantly said he would, while I whispered that I didn't even know who Shereen was. She waved a hand dismissively and told Shereen we were on our way. She hung up and gave Hassan back his phone as we started moving towards the corner of the street to find a taxi. I was walking next to Dalal, our arms touching as her body swung the way it always did, and I could feel my temperature slightly rise. I couldn't tell what was going through her head. Her voice carried a certain urgency, but there was a lightness to her step. Perhaps she'd had some wine at Soha's, I guessed, but she didn't necessarily seem drunk.

In the taxi, Hassan sat next to the driver, while I sat next to Dalal in the backseat. She poked my arm and gestured towards the dashboard with a grin. The driver had plastered a photo of a boy and a girl who I assumed were his children. They stood in a way that reflected an aesthetic embraced by the people of Cairo's poorer neighborhoods, the boy's chin resting on his fist, his elbow resting on his raised knee, his foot in turn resting on a red pouf in front of them, while his sister stood behind him, his hand on her shoulder. The background was a pale, blurred version of the foreground, and to the right of frame the boy appeared again in the same pose, this time on his own, from another angle: his chin against his hand, the solemn look in his eyes more pronounced, as though he were contemplating the prospect of peace in light of expanding settlement activities in the West Bank. It was surreal: the specters of the children across the photo, the odd composition, the eclectic space itself, and the hues in the backdrop, which ranged from light pink to bright blue. I laughed at the absurdity, and yet a strange beauty emanated amidst the repetition and the excess, which kept my eyes glued to the picture. It was its inner rhythm, perhaps, or how it was structured so that the girl's hand on her brother's shoulder echoed his chin on his fist, his elbow on his knee, his foot on the pouf. I looked at Dalal; I knew she'd appreciated the same things about it. We laughed softly, enveloped by an intense feeling I decided was gratitude — that we were who we

were, that that picture was plastered on the dashboard.

We got off in front of an old-looking building in Manial, near Abbas Bridge. Hassan suggested we buy some snacks before we went upstairs, and then he disappeared into a supermarket on the corner, leaving me and Dalal alone. She moved closer until she was standing next to me.

"I missed you," I said.

My relationship with Dalal confused me. I was still longing for Aya, but whenever I saw Dalal I couldn't control what I felt. The easiest way to describe it would be what Alberto Giacometti said after being hit by an automobile in 1938: "Something has happened to me." Something was indeed happening to me. I'd spend hours in her company and hardly feel the time pass. At night, consumed with grief over Aya's departure, I'd call her, and—although she'd been sleeping—she would soothe me: firmly, gently, her voice lush and deep, like the green of the Nile and the endless indigo of the Cairo night. I needed her the way nights needed company, yet I'd push her away sometimes, and she'd lash out. We were constantly negotiating our closeness. I'd tell her I was upset, that maybe it was better for her to run away from me and toward clearer things; she'd steadfastly answer that she was a big girl and didn't need me telling her what to do. I'd pull back and she'd dive in, then she'd withdraw, and I'd scurry back to her, terrified. She'd receive me with tenderness, and her certainty would scare me, so I'd wiggle away again. But she'd always bring me back. I exhausted her the way my mind exhausted me.

"Is that why you haven't called me in three days?"

"I want to tell you something."

"Tell me."

"Aya's seeing someone."

I hadn't planned on telling her, I just found myself saying it, and for a moment I was annoyed at the way I'd blurted it out. She looked hard into my face and said nothing. I lowered my gaze to the ground; she stroked the back of my head, burying her fingers in my hair. I glanced up to survey the street, looking out for any other souls lost in this wintry inferno. It was empty. I thought of resting my head on her chest, but Hassan showed up before I could. "Let's go," he yelled from a distance, and made his way into the building.

Shereen was waiting at the door to her apartment. She'd probably heard the elevator and had come out to see if it was us. Dalal hugged her and went in first, then Hassan.

"Hi, I'm — " I started to say, but before I could introduce myself she'd shaken my hand and started to walk in. I followed. It seemed that she'd just moved in: it smelled of fresh paint, and there were sparse furnishings, a dining table and chairs still covered in plastic, home appliances in their boxes and wrapped-up rugs in the corners. A large black-and-white portrait of a woman who appeared to be in her forties dominated the scene. Her short hair was partially covered with a scarf, her expression solemn. An ornamental wooden cross stood in another corner of the room.

"What would you like to drink?" Shereen asked. "There's vodka, rum, whiskey… I think we should go with whiskey, no? I have an unopened bottle of Glenfiddich."

She came back from the kitchen with four scotch glasses — two in each hand — and the bottle under one arm. I was about to tell her there were safer ways to carry them, but I noticed her eyes were red and her lips were trembling slightly. In that exact moment, the bottle fell to the floor, the crash echoing across the space. I watched the golden liquid seep through the old tiles as Shereen kept repeating: "I'm sorry, I'm so sorry, it's alright. I'm sorry." She knelt to clean up the broken glass, and when Hassan got up and tried to help her, she looked up swiftly and snapped: "Don't! I've got this." She brought out a broom and a dustpan and started sweeping the shattered pieces in fast, nervous movements, still muttering: "It's alright," before she suddenly burst into tears. Everyone was still and silent for a moment. Hassan had a bewildered look, while Dalal took the broom and dustpan from Shereen's hands, set them aside, and held her close. "What is it, habibti? What's wrong?" Shereen's sobs grew louder as Dalal continued to stroke her shoulders soothingly. That's when I noticed the glow on Dalal's face and realized that she, too, was crying.

Dalal was still wordlessly consoling Shereen, tears on her face, when I heard an abrupt whimper from behind me. I looked at Hassan, and he quickly buried his face in his arm, wiping his eyes. I couldn't believe it. I walked out to the balcony. That wasn't how I'd expected the night to go. I gazed out at Abbas Bridge, watching the incessant flow of cars in the distance. The city was heavy, like a dead elephant's corpse collapsed on a line of ants, and the air felt like rods of stillness lodged in my lungs. "I can't imagine what you must be thinking," Shereen's voice came from behind me. "We've only just met, and I'm suddenly blubbering like a child. I'm sorry."

"No, please," I said. "You wanted to spend some quality time with your friends. I'm sorry I imposed."

"Not at all. I'm glad you're here," she said. She stretched out her hand: "I'm Shereen."

"Hazem."

"I know."

"Well, I know who you are, too, but I thought we were pretending it's alright and nothing happened inside, and we're just meeting now."

She chuckled and took me by the arm back into the room. The floor was still glistening with whiskey, but the shards of glass were gone. Hassan was coming out of the bathroom while Dalal was trying to find a mop. Shereen disappeared into her bedroom for a minute, came back with a piece of hashish, and placed it on the table.

"At least we know this won't break," she said with a small smile.

Hassan brought out a pack of rolling paper from his pocket, but she shoved it aside and brought out a glass covered in a piece of plastic film that she'd pierced with two holes: one for the pin with the hash, the other to inhale.

The glass made its way around while Shereen turned on the BBC to watch the 10 o'clock news. It was filled with the usual catastrophes from around the world: a huge fire somewhere in Asia, a plane crash, a mass grave that had been discovered somewhere or other. Hassan made a joke about the apocalypse at which no one laughed, even though we were all pretty stoned. He looked offended. He rose from his seat on the floor and said it was getting late and he had to get home to his wife. He headed towards the door with a loud "see ya," and left.

As soon as he was gone, Shereen asked if we were hungry, and I said yes. She ordered a rucola pizza from a place in Zamalek. I objected, saying I didn't like my pizza with greens on top, but Dalal covered my hand with hers and said I would love this

"There's vodka, rum, whiskey…"

one in particular, before setting her head on my shoulder. Shereen hung up and lit a new piece of hash attached to the pin, then placed it inside the glass. She took a whiff before she put it back on the table, waiting for more smoke to gather. She turned to Dalal.

"Why did you bring that guy with you?"

"Bring him? You two were on the phone when I saw him."

"I know. Well, he's alright, I don't know. Do you know about that girl he's seeing?"

"What girl?"

"He's cheating on his wife with this girl, a theater director or something."

"I see."

"You see?"

"Well, what do you want me to do about it? Lecture him about right and wrong?"

"I don't know, but it's bullshit to be honest." She took another whiff from the hash glass, coughed, then stretched on the floor and went on: "It's bullshit. And the world is bullshit and I'm so over it and I really want to travel somewhere but I have no money and I don't even know what use it is leaving if I'm going to come back to Cairo anyway. What use is anything, really? We're alive, there's no cure for that."

Dalal said nothing, and neither did I. The only sound in the room was the BBC's weather forecast, predicting heavy rains in London and snow in Istanbul and another sunny day in Dubai. Dalal put her head on my thigh; I placed a hand on her shoulder. I looked into her eyes, overcome with tenderness, as smoke clouded the glass on the table.

The shrill sound of the doorbell shattered the moment. Dalal and Shereen each got up, rummaging for their wallets, while I opened the door, paid the delivery man and returned with the pizza. The hash had left us ravenous. I opened a can of beer, gulping down slice after slice, nearly unaware of the rucola leaves I hated. When we were done eating, Shereen got a phone call, after which she told us she was going to a house party in Garden City. She asked if we wanted to join, but neither Dalal nor I showed much enthusiasm.

Dalal asked if I was going back to Dokki, where I lived. I said yes, and she said she'd go back with me. Shereen told us she would be passing by Dokki to meet her dealer for a new bottle of Glenfiddich and that she could drop us on the way, but I said I wanted to walk. She took my hand, and this time brought me in for a kiss on each cheek. "I'm not crazy," she said in a low voice. "I just had a rough day."

I nodded in understanding, Dalal gave her one more hug, and we left.

It was drizzling when Dalal and I walked out of the building. I had always loved how it rained in Cairo. In a city of heat named "The Oppressor," I couldn't help but think the sky wept for us, the inhabitants of that sorrowful place. Dalal asked if we should get a taxi, I said no. We walked to the street corner and turned left onto Abbas Bridge, heading toward the Giza Corniche.

"So, how do you feel?" she asked me.

"About what?"

"Aya."

"I feel okay."

"Okay?"

I didn't want to talk about it. I pretended to rummage for my cigarettes in the pockets of my trousers, then my coat. I looked up to see a man selling chickpea soup staring at us. He leaned in and whispered something to one of his customers, who looked at us in turn with a yellowish grin on his face.

When you've lived in Cairo for years, you acquire a thick skin and a steady indifference toward anything that doesn't classify as an existential threat. That didn't, however, stop me from thinking I ought to walk up to that bastard and punch him in the nose. I glanced at Dalal. She, too, was looking at the chickpea seller, and to my surprise after meeting her eyes, the man and his miserable customer turned away, their staring session cut short. She reached out for my pack and pulled out a cigarette, placed it between her lips, then brought a lighter out of her purse. She lit her own cigarette before tilting it up to light mine with its smoldering tip. I leaned in and inhaled deeply, letting the smoke out in exasperation.

"I got the scholarship."

I looked up at her, astonished. She wasn't looking at me; her eyes were on a neon-lit boat making its way across the river on that late-winter night.

"When did you find out?"

"The day before yesterday."

"Why didn't you tell me?"

"I'm telling you now."

"Well, congratulations."

It was happy news, but she didn't look happy, and neither was I. I didn't know how to respond. I took another drag on my cigarette then flicked it over the bridge, half-finished.

"I'm surprised you didn't tell me as soon as they let you know."

"You weren't talking to me."

"It wasn't intentional. I just don't want things to get confusing."

"Confusing how?"

"Well, I don't mean confusing… I don't know."

She didn't persist and I didn't elaborate. We had descended the bridge and were walking down Nile Street towards Galaa Square, the grand river boats to our right, the French Embassy to our left. We'd been silent for a while when I heard a low meowing sound. I asked Dalal to stop as I tried to figure out where the weak squeals were coming from. I took a step backwards, scanned the sidewalk, and looked below the cars parked next to it until I noticed a motorcycle maneuver to avoid hitting a tiny bundle in the middle of the street. It was a kitten. Newborn, it seemed. She didn't appear to be able to move, even though she was still meowing. I took off my coat and looked both ways to make sure the road was clear. Right before I reached her, a car sped by and my heart leapt into my throat. I didn't know for sure if it had run her over, but I let out a loud curse, hurried towards the kitten, and wrapped her in my coat before walking back to the sidewalk.

Dalal was still there, unsure what was going on. I handed her my coat with the kitten inside it, took my phone out of my pocket, and dialed Fatma's number. She answered in a sleepy voice, wondering why the hell I was calling so late. I asked if she knew a vet clinic or a shelter that would be open at that hour. She said she'd make a few calls and get back to me. I took the coat from Dalal, crouched down to place it on the sidewalk, then opened it and peered at the kitten inside. The car had crushed her head. Her little brain was smashed, and one of her eyes dangled from its socket. My head was pound-ing, my heart racing in my chest. If I'd been faster, if I'd rushed across the street and tried to stop that car — perhaps I could've saved her. Or he would've hit me as well.

"Is she dead?" Dalal asked, and my phone rang at the same moment. It was Fatma. I told her the kitten was already dead and listened listlessly as she tried to console me. I hung up, walked to the concrete fence of the corniche, and emptied my coat of the kitten's small, mangled body. It fell among the rows of plants that lined the riverside nursery below.

"What are you going to do?" Dalal asked as I walked past her and onto the street.

"I'm going to find a taxi. I'm tired of walking."

"But you said you'd walk me home."

"No, I said I was walking home, and you said you'd come along."

"Alright. Suit yourself." Her voice was steely. She gathered her coat around her slender frame, turned around, and walked off, brisk and deliberate.

I saw a taxi approach and raised my arm to stop it. I was about to get in but then I gazed once more toward Dalal. I was surprised to see that she had stopped and stood a few steps away, looking back at me. I apologized to the taxi driver, and he swore at me and screeched off. I walked back to the fence where I'd thrown the kitten's body and sat down. In a few seconds, Dalal was standing before me, silent. I looked around to make sure no one was there, then rested my head against her stomach. She looked around to make sure no one was there, then put her hand against the back of my head and pulled me closer.

"It's alright, you can cry," she whispered.

Something crazy unraveled within me, something I'd been trying to keep locked in for what seemed like an eternity. I felt my heart crack like the windshield of a car that had just crashed into a wall. Hot tears spilled from my eyes and my sobs grew louder, wracking my entire body. Dalal didn't say a word, but she wiped her eyes and I could feel the wetness of her own tears when her hand moved back to my neck. I saw a passerby approach on the sidewalk, several plastic bags in each of his hands. He walked past, but then stopped in his tracks, looked back, and slowly made his way toward us. He looked at

Dalal: "What's wrong with him?"

"The cat died," Dalal answered solemnly.

The man fell silent for a second then said: "Sorry for your loss." He walked off, but it wasn't until a few long moments later that my tears stopped. I looked up at Dalal. "The cat died? Seriously?"

Then I laughed. It came out loud but heavy. I got up and gave her a playful shove, mimicking the sober look on her face as she sadly declared: "The cat died."

She began to laugh as well, uncontrollably. "Well, what did you want me to say?"

I wrapped an arm around her neck and pulled her gently towards me, then let her go with another light shove, and we started walking once more, still laughing.

"You're going to leave, and I won't have anyone to cry or go hysterical with," I said after we'd caught our breath.

"Maybe I won't."

"Why not?"

"I don't know, I'm still thinking about it."

"Thinking about what? Are you crazy? Go finish your Master's and find something better to do than dodging asshole officers at checkpoints and asshole men on the street."

"That's really naive, Hazem. It's not that easy."

"Nothing is, but most things are easier than life in Cairo."

"No. Nothing is easy."

I wanted to make a joke, but I knew she'd be able to tell I was using humor to cover my vulnerability. I looked at Dalal, studying the beauty of her face in the light emanating from the new Saudi Embassy — her wide brown eyes, her full lower lip, her delicate chin, the curve of her cheeks, the dimples that adorned them. My heart overflowed with tenderness. How generously she'd opened her world to me when my own had seemed so small. I remembered our first meeting after I'd broken up with Aya. Seven hours we'd spent together — I laughed and cried, I told jokes and tragic stories, she listened and the back of her hand brushed against mine as we walked side by side.

"I'm going to miss you," I said.

"I'm going to miss you too."

She took my hand in hers and squeezed it wordlessly. We crossed Galaa Square together as the baking aromas from Simonds filled the air. We were getting closer to her place. We made our way down al-Sadd al-Aali Street, past Bob Sushi, Alfa Market, KFC, the medical examination headquarters for Egyptians hoping to migrate to Kuwait, the Spanish Cultural Center. When we reached Quick, she asked me to wait outside while she bought a bar of chocolate. I leaned against a parked car and looked out across Vinni Square. I watched an ambulance speed towards Shabrawishi Hospital, my own heart speeding in my chest. When she came out of the store with her chocolate, we continued on our way toward her building through the numerous circles of teenagers scattered around the square, and all the while I was wondering at what point I should leave her. I expected her to invite me up, but I wasn't entirely ready for that. It wouldn't be the first time for me in her apartment, I'd gone up a few times throughout that past month, the last being a week or so ago. She had been sick, so I told her I'd pass by and picked up a kilo of bananas on my way. "You shouldn't have," she'd said when she saw it, and I told her it was good for her cold. "Oranges are," she'd replied with a smile, but she took the bag anyway.

"I should go home," I told her now.

"Why?"

"You don't want me to?"

"No, I don't. Come up."

"I'm tired."

"Me too. But come up."

I didn't want to flat-out refuse, so I made a couple more excuses, but when she insisted, I told myself there was no harm in it. What's the worst that could happen? The effect of the weed had almost completely worn off. I could stay for twenty minutes or so. Dalal switched on the light at the entrance to the building, then turned to me with her finger against her lips, signaling me to be quiet. She started to ascend the stairs and I soundlessly followed. We stopped for a second when we heard a door open and a man shuffle out with a trash bag. He placed it in the bin in front of his apartment and walked back in, the door closing with a bang behind him. We stayed still until the lights went off, then continued on our way up.

Her apartment was a lot warmer than the street. I headed to

"I'm tired."

the bathroom as soon as we entered, took off my coat, and relieved my full bladder. When I walked out, Dalal was standing on her bed, her back to the door, trying to reach the top shelf of her closet. I was admiring the beauty of her backside when she turned and said, in her bossiest tone, "Will you be useful for once and grab me that blanket up there?"

I sat on the floor and looked up at her with a smile, intentionally provocative. She climbed down and pulled me by the arm. I pushed her with a laugh and her head hit the headboard. A small moan escaped her as her hand flew to her head, and I hurried to her, touching the spot she'd been rubbing. It was already starting to swell. "I'm so sorry," I whispered.

She pushed my hand with a smile and walked out of the room. As I reached up for the blanket, I heard her ask if I wanted something to drink. I asked if she still had that peach tea from last time, she said yes, and came back and said no. I followed her to the kitchen, where she stood in front of the stove as water boiled in the kettle. My body rubbed against hers as I leaned in to open one of the cupboards. She gave me a pointed look. "What?" I chuckled. "Your kitchen's too small!"

I went through endless packets of herbal teas before I decided on hibiscus and cinnamon. I put the tea bag in a mug, and the smell warmed my head as she poured in the steaming water. She asked if I wanted any sugar; I said I wanted honey. She raised an eyebrow. "I'm trying to quit sugar," I explained. She smiled as she stirred the honey in my drink and asked me to take hers along and go up to the roof. I carefully picked up the clay mugs and followed her up the steps.

It was cold, but she made a small fire in a broken steel bowl that had probably been used for mixing cement and left behind by construction workers. I placed the mugs on a small makeshift table and plopped down on the lonely swing next to the fire. She threw the blanket over my head and giggled softly as she sat down next to me. I spread the blanket over us, and we sat in silence for a few moments, gazing into the fire.

"The cold is much worse in New York," she said.

"But the heaters are good."

"But I won't be able to take long walks at dawn like I do here. I would freeze."

"But you'll have a functioning sidewalk to walk on during the rest of the day."

"If Cairo had proper sidewalks, just proper sidewalks, it would be beautiful."

"And a Central Park."

"And a Metropolitan, while we're at it."

"I'd do without the Met, just proper sidewalks and a good park."

She rested her head on my shoulder, I rested my head on hers. Her hand tightened around mine. I lifted my head and gazed down at her. She was inching toward me. I kissed her forehead in an attempt to avoid the moment, but her eyes locked on mine. I kissed her on the mouth then, slowly but passionately; she kissed me back with a fervor to match. I kissed her again — once, twice, ten times, until a single thought crystallized in my head. I wanted to sleep in my bed. Well, no, it wasn't really my bed that I longed for, but a clear head, unburdened by the weight of the world's arrangements. I was dreading the moment when I'd have to leave, in a few hours or tomorrow afternoon or the evening of the day after. How would I go about getting dressed? Would I kiss her on my way out? What would we talk about? The future? The past? The present? How would we avoid time, politics, distance, love? At a more basic level, how would I close the door behind me when I left? A sudden chill ran through me, and I wasn't sure if it was the cold or the fear that was consuming me.

"I have to go."

She lifted her head with a puzzled look. She tried to kiss me again, but I stopped her this time and repeated what I'd said, looking straight into her eyes: "I have to go."

I scrambled to my feet, knocking down our mugs as I rushed out. I sighed and turned back to at least clean up that mess, but as I bent down to pick them up, I heard a soft whimper. Dalal's face was buried in her hands, and she was crying. I sat down next to her and placed a hand on her shoulder with no idea what to say. She was sobbing now, I tried to hold her, but she pushed me away.

"Go, now."

She was still crying, but I knew what I had to do. I walked towards the door with steady steps, opened it, and left.

The moment I was out of the apartment, I realized I'd forgotten my coat in the bathroom. I stupidly considered going back in to ask for it, but instantly decided it was a bad idea. I placed my ear to the door, trying to figure out what she was doing now. Dalal would go to bed upset, and she probably wouldn't talk to me — not tomorrow, not in a week, not ever. I closed my eyes, my head still against her door, and it seemed as though I'd stay like that for a lifetime, but the dawn call to prayer rose up from a nearby mosque, reminding me that it was time to leave. I walked heavily down the stairs. When I made it to the first floor, a cat was clawing through one of the garbage cans. She looked up nervously, and I wished I could find a way to assure her that I would do her no harm, but she'd already fled past me to the ground floor, out the gate, and onto the street.

At home, I sat on a couch Aya and I had bought together from IKEA. She'd always referred to it as the first piece of furniture in "our marriage." It also happened to be the last. I'd asked her to take it with her when she moved out, but she said she no longer liked the color. I never even liked the couch to begin with, but, that day, my arguments had waned against her excitement. And so I ended up with a couch I hated in my otherwise empty living room. I hadn't turned on the lights, but a stubborn beam flitted into the room through the closed curtains, sabotaging my darkened mood. I reached for my laptop and an ashtray, planning to watch some porn in an effort to relax and fall asleep. The screen lit up and a notification in the lower right corner told me I had a new email message. It was Aya. I felt a sudden burning in my stomach and an overwhelming urge to go to the bathroom. When had she sent it? An hour ago, the email said. Where had I been? Carrying a dead kitten to the side of the road? Crossing the square with Dalal, hand in hand? I snapped my laptop shut, paced across the living room for a minute, then went back to the couch and opened it again. I lit a cigarette and clicked on the message.

So today I read about the panopticon gaze in Kundera's novel, how you are always being watched, very closely; by the government, by your lover, by someone. You are either the see-er or the seen. I also read about how you

can hear the ocean wherever you are on the planet. The waves are named 'Love' waves. I'm not joking. It's named after someone and I can't remember the details. Last night a friend wrote to me about how we're engaged in a culture of nihilism and aggression, and yet we expect to be provided with the exact opposite (like we deserve it), or as if we even have the capacity for it — that is, kindness and meaningfulness and tenderness. What's your favorite color? Do you remember the scene in Short Term 12 where each one would describe how they feel with a color and what it stands for? Green: just fine. Grey: whatever. Etc. I don't know what stands for what, but I'm always blue. Blue in how I feel and what I want and where I wind up. My eyes are a magnet for anything blue. We are poetic but life isn't, or vice versa. I'm blabbering. What was it that I wanted to say? I met a guy, nothing like you, not in any meaningful way. I was sitting with a colleague at work and she was talking about how miserable she is and how pointless her days are. There's no end to the possibilities of the human condition. He came along, and it felt right, just as it should feel. Do I care if you hate me? I do, but I won't stop you. Today I found out that the police are looking for someone I met back in November, in Sinai. What I remember about him is that he was very handsome and had a very attractive British accent. What do we do with all this information? What if I don't have the stomach for it? You live in a place that is unbelievably brutal. Shameless. Yet it is unbearably familiar. I remember when we talked about Cairo and when you told me about the old lady at the pool. You are poetic, Cairo isn't. Or Cairo is and you aren't.

I love you, Zuzu.

Is there a landscape big enough to fit the everyday? To fit the self? The malaise? The confusion? The information? The fragility? The beauty?

You know what's the best part about Peter Pan? The Lost Boys.

Stay well,
Aya

I wondered if I should reply. Aya had found someone new, there was no doubt about it now. I was angry, extremely so, but I also felt clear. Composed. I looked around the living room. It seemed bigger somehow. Her memory had been a physical presence, eating up my space. I was nowhere near sleepy. Should I reply? No. It was over. I knew she would be waiting for my answer — a nice, poetic letter like the ones we used to exchange before we got together. I had no energy to be nice or otherwise. We'd finally become two, Aya. Whatever had brought us together had come to an end; the paths that we'd once tread together, we must now tread alone.

I was consumed with thoughts of Dalal. I could see her in my head, her face in her hands as she cried. I left my seat on the couch with her image still before me. I lay my head on my pillow, and still, it wouldn't leave me. I stayed in bed for half an hour, thinking of her soothing voice, remembering the time I'd woken her up crying because I missed Aya so much. That night, I'd told her that perhaps it was wise for us not to see each other for a while, for fear that we'd be swept up in something we couldn't handle, and then we'd promised each other we'd remain friends no matter what happened. I got out of bed, my head filled with noise. I put on a sweater and walked out onto the street. I passed a fuul cart, a vegetable stand, a tourist bus. I crossed one street after the next and in my haste stumbled onto a brick, to the delight of a group of young girls on their way to school, whose laughter followed me down the road. I didn't know how much time had passed when I found myself in front of Dalal's building.

The gate was closed, and before it sat the same cat that had run away from me the night before. She meowed as though asking for something. To my relief, the gate opened when I pushed it. I walked in and looked over my shoulder to see the cat creep in stealthily behind me. I flew up the stairs and stopped at Dalal's door. I put my ear against the door as I had only a few hours ago; I rang the bell and heard her approach. I could feel her standing on the other side of the door, and I knew she'd looked through the peephole and seen me before I heard her move back inside. I rang the bell again. I thought she wasn't coming back, but the door opened suddenly, and my coat hit me in the face, and then it closed again and I heard the lock

click, but not before I glimpsed her in a bathrobe, her hair dripping. I continued to ring the bell, insistently. She opened the door, tentatively this time, but kept the chain lock hooked. I saw part of her face through the narrow slit; her eyes were red and swollen, possibly from crying, or maybe from lack of sleep. I wanted to take her face in my hands, but her glare told me she'd bite my fingers off if I tried.

"What do you want?"

"I want us to talk."

"There's nothing to talk about."

"Why?"

"Because we can't keep playing games anymore."

"I don't want to play games."

"Then what do you want?"

I would have been lying if I told her I knew what I wanted. But I did know—I wanted to rest my head on her thigh, I wanted her to embrace me the way she had the night before on the side of the road. I wanted to tell her a thousand random stories about myself that I hadn't yet told her, and to listen to a thousand random stories about her that she hadn't yet told me.

"I'm scared," I said.

"So am I!"

"Do you want me to leave?"

"Well, do you want to come in?"

"Yes."

She closed the door abruptly and, for a minute, I didn't think she was going to open it again. I wondered if I knew what I was doing. I was sure of one thing: I didn't want to go home; not now — perhaps not ever. Perhaps home was wherever Dalal was. What was I supposed to do now that she'd slammed the door in my face?

I was heading toward the stairs when I heard the rattle of the chain. I turned around. The door was open, but Dalal wasn't there. I stood at the threshold and gazed in toward the balcony at the opposite end of the apartment. The sunlight was so bright I had to look away. I closed my eyes, walked in, and shut the door behind me.

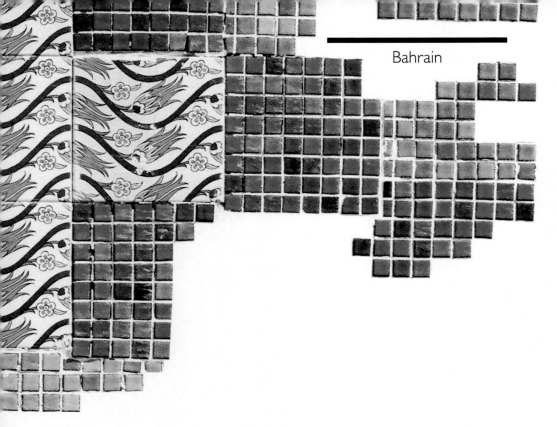

Waves
of the Future

By **Rawan Maki** with input from **Nidal Khalaf**

Tiles: Rawan Maki

Translated
by Rawan Maki

We "reclaim" the land from water, taking back what was never given,
worshiping our own footsteps, which replace the water's sheen.
Perhaps, if we tread more lightly, the shore could erase a few.

The Gulf's waters remain wise—
they know where to meet the shore on a desert island—
through ebb, and flow,
an equilibrium—always dynamic—a conversation,
and when we come to meet the future,
we realize the future is here; it's been happening all along.

When we come to meet ourselves,
we peel off layers, put on even more,
the feminine palm leaves and masculine bark from each root are
not genderless! But gender-ful, with the beauty of both contained in
your own layers, patchwork of yourself.

They will come undone, only to be re-purposed.
Ask not why each wave is there,
but where the ocean moves as a whole, and
trust that, in its vastness, there is direction.

Vastness is not endless, not empty,
it is rich in vastness—
grasp the vastness—weave it into yourself—
and you will no longer see anything else:
yes, the future is here.

Sip the tea now, warm your hands, and
as for the set of cards in your grip right now:
admire them,
stack them! Shuffle, deal,
re-use them.

Home is where you start, but also all the places where you feel yourself
"becoming."
We are all recycled versions of ourselves, magnified by each re-use.

كوكلجم

'How Delightful Your Arrival Would Be'

a Moroccan malhun poem

مازين

Historic malhun photo bought off the street in Essaouira.

By Melanie Magidow

The history of *malhun*—a deeply symbolic and eclectic genre of sung poetry—begins in the fifteenth century, in Tafilalt (in today's eastern Morocco), prior to the establishment of the national border that separates Morocco and Algeria. First composed in hand-written songbooks, which circulated among urban artists, craftspeople, and Sufi groups, *malhun* distinguished itself from other Moroccan regional traditions by the breadth of its social and geographical appeal.

A collection of malhun poems edited by Abdel Samad Belkabir.

By the eighteenth and nineteenth centuries, *malhun* had become a symbol of the country's increased unification, and came to represent Arab pride and resistance to foreign domination, i.e., Ottoman, French, Spanish, and British rule. (Note that while malhun has also been composed in southern and western Algeria, where it contributed to the development of raï music, it has not become symbolic of national unity in Algeria as it has in Morocco.)

While still composed and performed by contemporary poets, singers, and musicians, the heyday of this genre falls between the seventeenth to nineteenth centuries. (Significantly, this is the pre-colonial era, meaning before the French Protectorate, which officially administered Morocco from 1912 to 1956.) And yet this centuries-old musical genre continues to attract listeners and readers to this day, namely through intimate gatherings, public concerts, mass media, and printed books.

This broad modern audience swelled in the 1960s thanks to the Nass El Ghiwane cultural movement, which reintroduced many beloved classics of Moroccan *malhun*; the eponymous musical group behind this movement notably spearheaded the national rediscovery and reinvention of artistic forms associated with the Independence generation and with pre-French Protectorate society.

Malhun has come to appeal to most Moroccan publics, including audiences fluent in French and/or Amazigh languages, and is now a mainstay in weddings, as well as at public concerts and festivals. This comes no doubt from its unique place in the literary and musical arts in Morocco, distinguished by its long written history, priority of language over musical accompaniment, wide range of sub-genres, and use of spoken Arabic. *Malhun*'s origin in Tafilalt, the birthplace of the royal family, and its incorporation of both "folk" and "classical" genres, provide additional appeal.

A few technical notes: The term '*malhun*' also refers to the musical accompaniment. Students in *malhun* classes at musical conservatories usually learn to perform malhun poems first by keeping time, clapping, or using *ta'rījas* (hand-held hour-glass-shaped clay drums). At public concerts, musical ensembles (*jawq*, pl. *ajwāq*) may include ten or twenty members, and typically use drums and stringed instruments (*ūd* / lute, *rabāb* / fiddle, *kamānja* / violin).

Textual features of malhun poetry include meter, rhyme, intertextuality, lexicon, imagery, and language varieties. Poets of malhun could hypothetically use any language. For example, even though malhun is thought of as a genre composed in Moroccan Arabic, there is also Judeo-Arabic malhun poetry, written in Hebrew characters; the genre has also been influenced by Amazigh culture (and vice versa). Malhun poetry includes several sub-genres: *madīḥ* / praise, and its inverse, hijāʾ / invective; lyric poetry on wine (*khamriyya*), love (*ghazal*), and nature (*rabīʿiyya*); laments *(rithāʾ)*; political appeals (*jifriyya*); narratives (*tarjama*); comic debates; and religious themes (usually *tawassul*).

The following excerpt comes from a well-known poem by the most famous Moroccan *malhun* poet, ʿAbd al-Qādir al-ʿAlamī (Meknes, 1742-1850). It is a love poem, but it also draws on Sufi poetry (Sufism is a mystical branch of Islam) in terms of language and imagery. The sea appears in Sufi texts as a symbol of the great unknown (a sea of knowledge, a sea of love, ultimately symbolizing the infinite divine). There is no contradiction between human love and divine love; they blend together in Sufi texts and the works they inspire. In this poem, the original Arabic includes end rhyme (you can see how the same letter is repeated at the end of every line and half-line in the Arabic text). The excerpt consists of three parts: the refrain and verses 4 and 5, which are the two final stanzas of the poem.

Refrain

How delightful your arrival would be
      my radiant moon... if it weren't for your aloofness
and the enviers' talk
      and the chaperone who holds you back

Fourth Verse

I cut through your barrier
      and you fell from your heavens
I foiled your enchantments
      after your chaperone used to protect you
I endured your seas,
      entered your waves, and drank your water
I captured your ships at night,
      and not one voyager could save you
I fought your infantry,
      and the army that failed you was defeated
I conquered your cavalry
      and my sword could have taken your life
I routed your armies
      who were fighting to protect you
And the servants of your rows,
      hearing your wish as their command.

Fifth Verse

I'm beholden to your light,
      overwhelmed by your brightness
I've seen your stars—
      be the crown in the presence of a king
I've enjoyed your happiness
      When you treated me like your brother
Or like your loved one
      My image, at a glance was enough for you
But it's the way you are,
      and no one can change you.
From the state of your faults,
      only my Creator will worsen or cure you.
In the gardens of your courtyard
      peace and greetings I convey
their good fragrance, with tones of musk,
      for the great people of art and for you

Use the QR code below to listen to the poem set to music.

How Delightful Your Arrival Would Be, *Abd al-Qadir al-Alami*

الحربة	ما زين وصولك	يا البدر الساني لولا جفاك
	وكلام حسودك	والرقيب اللي داير بك

القسم الرابع	مزقت حجوبك،	بسيف شعري وهويت من سماك
	وبطلت سحورك،	بعد كان رقيبك يحميك
	شكيت بحورك،	دخلت بين لماجك وشربت ماك
	وغنمت سفونك،	ولا قدر من يسري يفديك
	حاربت جنودك،	راح مهزوم الجيش اللي غواك
	وقهرت خيولك،	وكان سيفي غادي يبريك
	وهزمت جيوشك،	والطرارد منصوبة في حماك
	وعبيد صفوفك،	سامعين الامر طاعة ليك

القسم الخامس	زاوكت فنورك،	منين خجلوا نجلاتي من ضياك
	ونظرت شموسك،	كن تاج فحضرت ملك
	وغنمت سرورك،	منين كنتي دايرني كيف خاك
	ولا محبوبك،	صورتي بالنظرة تكفيك
	لكن مكتوبك،	لا غنا يتصرف شاين عطاك
	من حال عيوبك،	خالقي يبليك ويشفيك
	فحدايق روضك،	السلام نهيبو طيبو شداك
	بعبير مسوكك،	للدهات أهل الفن وليك

If Not for the Mediterranean

Ibrahim Abdel Meguid's *Clouds Over Alexandria* is a cartography of past and present set in Egypt's second-largest city. The novel follows the lives of a group of friends in mid-1970s Alexandria, where different shades of cosmopolitanism appear through the eyes of the novel's core characters, each of whom has a distinct connection to the city. Nadir, a promising young poet, navigates his relationship with his girlfriend, Yara, along with the tension of the city's ideological differences. Bishr Zahran, a magazine editor and Communist recruit, is a social renegade full of mordant sarcasm and lust. The novel is cinematic, bringing the reader close to the pulse of Alexandria through snatches of its history. A tale of desire,

friendship, and social revolution, this "documentary" novel sketches a portrait of contemporary Egyptian identity – even though it is set in 1975, during the time of President Anwar Sadat.

In Kay Heikkenen's translation, the sentences are sonic, textured with musicality. Snippets of songs from radio and film (such as Muhammad Abdel Wahhab's "The Night was Calm") and allusions to notable singers (Edith Piaf, Abdel Halim Hafiz, Dean Martin) set the mood for reading. Some of the pages could be set as scores to songs, and an attentive
reader can hear the poems and music that underlie the plot. ◆

By Tópé Salaudeen-Adégòkè

BRIAN ENO — FRENCH CATALOGUES

(Variation on the 'Canon in D Major' by Johann Pachelbel)

The novel opens with a wide-angle shot, taking stock of world events and situations happening in Egypt before centering on the individual lives of everyday people, as if to assert their place in the annals of history. Brian Eno's ambient adagio is a soothing accompaniment to usher the reader into the novel. Its subtle repetitions merge the landscape of Alexandria of the novel with its people living their everyday lives such that they become one – this is one of the central themes of the novel.

on the sea-shore in Jaffa
J. Benor-Kalter

TCHAIKOVSKY — 'MARCHE SLAVE, OP 49'

FELA — 'CONFUSION' AND 'ZOMBIE'

These tracks are among the most popular of the Afrobeat music genre. And they are Fela's, the social critic who endlessly parodied the both social ills and the tyranny of Nigerian military dictatorship. These two tracks are laid with heavy instrumentations. 'Confusion' helps build the tension as the stakes rise, and then 'Zombie', which is a mock-heroic of martial music, hints at state-security surveillance and military oppression that characterizes both the novel and the Sadat era.

This track came early in the plot, when Nadir is summoned by state security to be questioned about whether he holds a political ideology contrary to the State's. "At that moment in his room Tchaikovsky's Marche Slave filled the air around him, coming from the radio. As usual he was surprised at the announcer who called it 'March of the Slaves,' not realizing that 'Slav' is the name of a people and does not mean "slaves…" This misunderstood orchestra stands in for the voice of the masses, and the historical backdrop of the composition comes soon after Nadir has received his summons to appear at the State Security headquarters.

LEONARD BERNSTEIN; NEW YORK PHILHAR-MONIC ORCHESTRA

—

'ROMEO AND JULIET FANTASY OVERTURE, TH 42'

This is another song to build and elaborate the romantic texture of the plot, as well as the secrecy and uncertainty that dog it. From the orchestra's melodramatic intervals, one can get a sense of the plot's sub-conflict: the precarity of a closet affair between a man and a woman in 1970s Egypt, and the longing ache of the lovers. It is also a reminder of the liberalism and secularism of parts of Alexandria, standing against the conservatism of religious doctrines.

BOB DYLAN — 'CAN'T HELP FALLING IN LOVE'

There are many steamy romantic relationships in the plot – sometimes, complicated. The lyrics on this track are a paean to the lovebirds: "Like a river flows surely to the sea/ Darling, so it goes, some things were meant to be."

Saffi (Marokko) Palmen von Sidi Busid.

BEAUTIFUL NUBIA — 'WE LIVE HERE TOO'

Alexandria is for all, regardless of political orientation, national status, or ethnic coloration. This particular track reinforces this claim and the danger of xenophobic sentiments against the Greeks. It encourages people to stake claim to their city and compliments the theme of Alexandria's cosmopolitanism. The gentle refrain of Beautiful Nubia and the flourish of trumpets that accompany it is a gentle reminder that minority opinions should also be heard and respected.

NAS AND DAMIAN MARLEY — 'TRIBES AT WAR'

'Tribes at War' rings with the complications that arise from ideological differences and also heightens the tension of the novel: brothers fighting brothers, divided along lines of ideological and religious difference. The tempo of the song and its lyrics echo what Abdel Meguid achieves in the mind of the reader. The strife and striving between the secular and spiritual. The song echoes the similar tension in American society.

NAJAT AL SAGHIRA — 'سكة العاشقين'

"Politics doesn't kill, love is what kills." These are the words of Nadir's mother near the end, after she shares her own love story, resonating with the polyrhythm of Al Saghira's "The Lovers' Path": "O night, o night, o night, o night, I am a lover who tells tales."

SALIF KEITA — 'FOLON'

The novel's final chapter is best read solemnly, because it is a long emotive poem with a tessitura appeal. The plot winds down in a heartrending denouement that leaves a question about fidelity suspended in the same Odyssean imperfectness that also appears in a recent Nigerian novel, An Orchestra of Minorities, by Chigozie Obioma. The passionate vocals of Salif Keita on this track are both golden and somber, which makes it a perfect background to the reading of the poem by Nadir, which reads in part: "He said to me: / If it were not for the Mediterranean sea/ there would have been no Odyssey/ I said to him: / Odysseus returned /and our labyrinth began."

Illustrations from
Firas Makes the Sea,
by the Egyptian
artist Nabil Taj.

Whose is the sea?

Liana Badr, Firas Makes a Sea
Taghreed Najjar, Against the Tide
Sonia Nimr, Wondrous.
Journeys in Amazing Lands

By M Lynx Qualey

In children's stories, the sea is—almost invariably—a place of adventure and escape. It's home to pirates and whales, mermaids and submarines. It's a place of magic, where the real and the unreal conjoin. But while magical themes are often shared across cultures, the "real" of children's literature differs. In Palestinian stories for young people, the fantasy of the sea co-exists with displacement, checkpoints, societal disapproval, gunboats, exile, and hunger.

In Taghreed Najjar's *Sitt al-Kol* (2013), the thin blue ribbon of Mediterranean that borders the Gaza Strip is the setting of a harsh reality and, nonetheless, magic. *Sitt al-Kol*, which the author prefers to call *Against the Tide* in English, was Najjar's first novel for young adults, following decades of picture books, and it was shortlisted for Arabic literature's big YA prize. The book is based on the real story of Gazan teen Madeleine Kolab, who rather prosaically took over her father's fishing business after he became too ill to manage it.

In *Against the Tide*, our hero is 15-year-old Yusra. Her older brother has been killed; her younger brother too small to pitch in. As in many of Najjar's books, a macho Palestinian patriarch struggles to adjust to reduced circumstances. Yusra's father must adjust to life in a wheelchair, after losing the use of his legs when a tunnel beneath the border with Egypt collapsed. Yusra's mother, alone, struggles to find enough for the family to eat. Until Yusra steps forward to help provide for her family.

Despite this grim backdrop, this book does contain magic, which of course resides in that slim ribbon of water that runs between the shore of daily life and the wall of Israeli gunboats that sits a few miles out, hemming in Gaza's 4000-odd fishing boats. The magic here is that Yusra succeeds in fixing up her father's old fishing boat; not only that, she gets her family to agree to let her go catch fish for their livelihood, her father swayed by how magically Yusra and her friends have fixed up and repainted his boat.

But both on shore and at sea, bossy reality intervenes. The shore-bound tittle-tattles don't approve of Yusra's nontraditional employment. And when our young heroine takes the boat too far out, in search of a better catch, she runs right into Israeli gunboats. The space for magic is hardly wider than a balance beam: there is no room here for romance, scarcely enough for a girl to stretch her arms and throw a net. Yet Yusra prevails.

- «قَدْ يَنْقُصُ هَذَا الْبَحْرَ لَوْنٌ أَزْرَقُ !»

جَاءَ «فِرَاسٌ» بِزُجَاجَةٍ مِنَ الْحِبْرِ الْأَزْرَقِ ، وَصَبَّها
فَوْقَ الْمَاءِ . ثُمَّ حَرَّكَهُ بِيَدَيْهِ لِيَصْنَعَ أَمْوَاجاً .

وَعِنْدَمَا نَظَرَ «فِرَاسٌ» إِلَى الْمَاءِ
الْأَزْرَقِ ، قَالَ :

- «لَيْسَ هَذَا بَحْراً !» .

This tiny slip of Mediterranean stands in sharp contrast to an earlier incarnation, set some 500 years ago, in Sonia Nimr's *Rihlat Ajeeba fi al-Bilad al-Ghareeba* (2014), a winner of Arabic YA's top prize. *Wondrous Journeys in Amazing Lands*—the title a clear nod to Ibn Battuta's *A Gift to Those Who Contemplate the Wonders of Cities and the Marvels of Traveling*—is an alt-Ibn Battuta; instead of a wealthy Moroccan man who sets out for hajj, a clever Palestinian girl named Qamr leaves home in search of adventure. The first time she catches sight of the Mediterranean, also on the Gaza shore, she is enthralled. "It was the first time I smelled the salt, heard the sound of the waves, and saw the white foam clinging to the beach before the wave draws it away, only to throw it back again."

But this feminist fable quickly veers into a rockier demi-realism. Qamr is captured by brigands and taken away from her beloved sea; she ends up a slave to Egypt's royal family. After she escapes, she travels to the Moroccan coast to study with a famous scholar. Here, like Yusra, she must defy the gender roles of her day. At first, the famed scholar refuses to let a girl listen in on his lessons. Yet eventually he lets her hide behind a curtain, as long as she remains silent. Naturally, it isn't long before our fierce Qamr blurts out an answer when the men get everything wrong. She is forced to set out again. But where? The sea, of course.

Here, in the time before passport control and the Sykes-Picot, the Mediterranean belongs not to any particular nation-state, but to whomever is strong or clever enough to master it. And so, dressed as a boy, Qamr snags a berth on a pirate vessel. She not only manages to stay alive through countless adventures, but she also uses the healing skills she's learned from books to bind up her fellow pirates after battle. She marries and settles down. Yet she cannot stay in one place, and, when she sets out, a storm dashes Qamr's ship to pieces. For a Palestinian girl, the sea before borders is magic, high adventure, and excitement. But it's also grim loss and the struggle to hope again.

While Yusra's sea comes in the middle of the book, and Qamr's journey ends there, the earlier story of Firas, in *Firas Makes a Sea* (1984), begins with sea. This young boy of five or six has lost his magical sea—or rather, the sea has been stolen from him—and now he must recreate it.

This picture book by Palestinian novelist Liana Badr, illustrated by Nabeel Taj, is only a few pages long. Yet, they are enough for Badr to create a bright, magical story and suggest a darker reality beneath it.

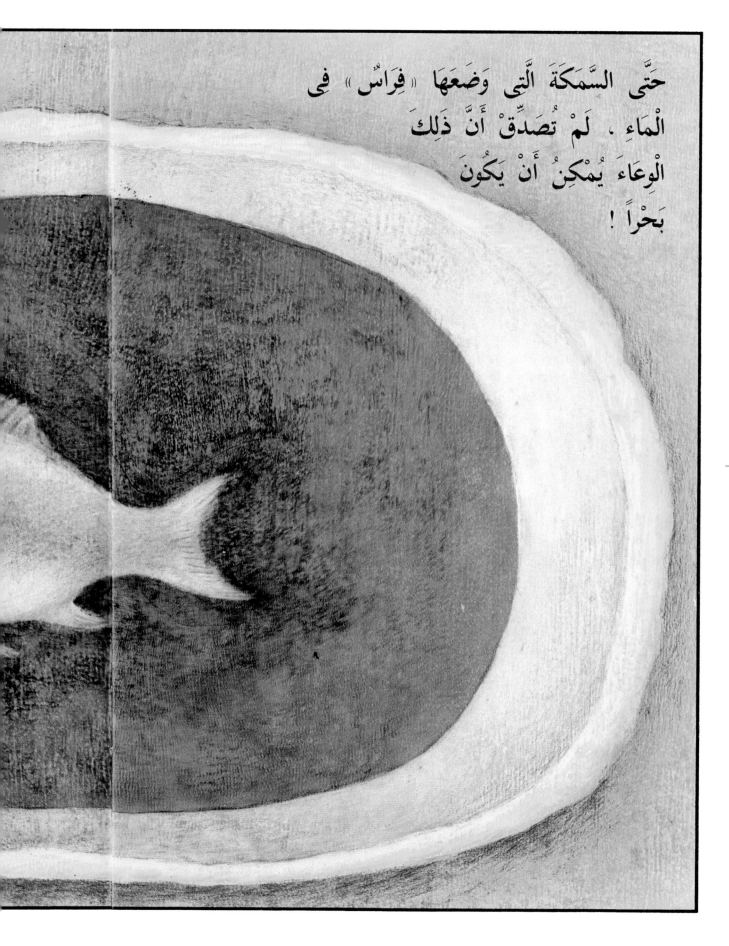

حَتَّى السَّمَكَة الَّتِي وَضَعَهَا «فِرَاسٌ» فِي الْمَاءِ ، لَمْ تُصَدِّقْ أَنَّ ذَلِكَ الْوِعَاءَ يُمْكِنُ أَنْ يَكُونَ بَحْرًا !

The reader knows little about Firas's life before. We learn that his whole family—apart from him—had seen and known the sea before they were forced to emigrate. Tenderly, the family described the sea for Firas: its gentle blue that shaded into the blue of the sky; the soft white of the beach, where footprints would be stamped in place until waves came along, erasing them; the way waves would turn the sand back into a blank page. Firas's family tells him how the waves used to whisper, day and night, and how the moon would be reflected on the sea. They tell about dreams of giant ships heading off to distant countries, full of mysterious secrets.

We learn all this on the first double page as Firas stares out at us, his gaze intent and direct, as if he needs us to understand him. Then he sets to his task: reclaiming the sea. First, he pumps water into a basin to make a sea. But though he pumps and pumps, no magic appears, and he does not make a sea. So Firas goes out for salt, then blue ink, then sand, then shells. But the magic never comes.

In the end, Firas is confronted with the realization that nothing can make his small basin into a sea. He knows that the true, great sea will continue to call him. "And," the book ends, "despite all the difficulties, he will return to it."

But how? On its placid blue surface, this could mean that Firas will triumph over the checkpoints and stamps and tanks that stand between him and the sea; that he will press his footprints into the sand, listen to its magic whispers, and join its blue-on-blue. But beneath that possibility is another one, hinted at by the book's final page—an endless expanse of blues, broken only by the yellow disc of the sun. Firas, who may never again reach the sea of his parents, may find magic by building this sea from stories.

Today, thirty-five years after the book's publication, Firas would be a man in his forties. Perhaps he is in prison, like the father in Walid Daqqa's landlocked YA novel, *The Oil's Secret Tale*. Perhaps he's deceased, like the father in Sonia Nimr's time-traveling YA fantasy *Thunderbird*. Or perhaps Firas has snuck past the Separation Wall and works in Israel, like the young protagonist in Taghreed Najjar's *Mystery of the Falcon's Eye*. Perhaps Firas sees the sea every day. Perhaps, despite all the difficulties, he has magicked himself the right to swim in it, with his pudgy-faced children. We can certainly dream it for him.

He is, after all, a fiction. ◆

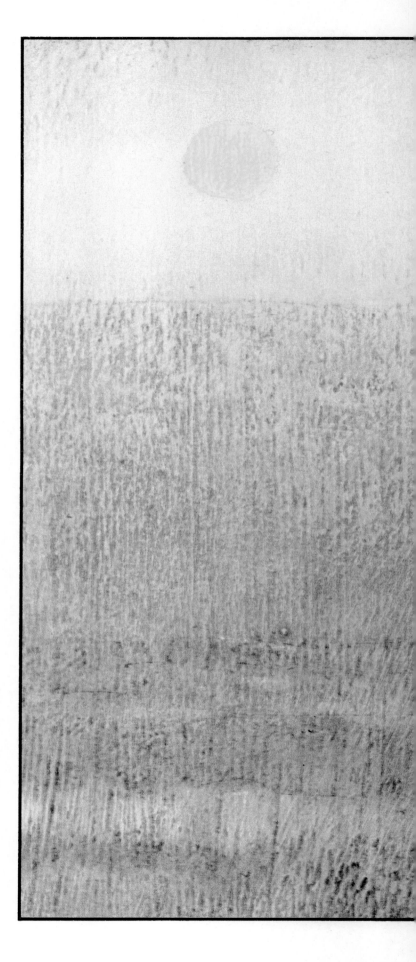

عَرَفَ «فِرَاسٌ» أَنَّهُ لا يَسْتَطِيعُ أَنْ يَصْنَعَ
مِنْ كُلِّ هَذِهِ الْأَشْيَاءِ بَحْراً . وأَنَّ الْبَحْرَ
الْكَبِيرَ الْحَقِيقِيَّ سَيَظَلُّ يُنَادِيهِ ، وأَنَّهُ سَيَعُودُ
إِلَيْهِ بِرَغْمِ كُلِّ الصُّعُوبَاتِ .

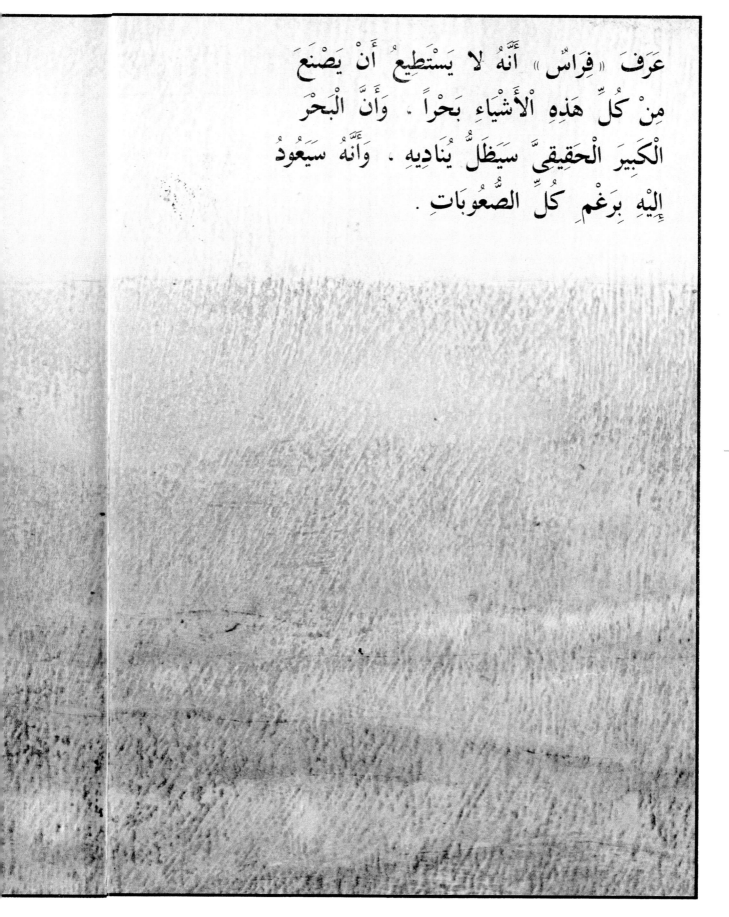

Diaries of an Overseas Student

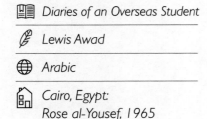

📖 *Diaries of an Overseas Student*

🖋 *Lewis Awad*

🌐 *Arabic*

🏠 *Cairo, Egypt:*
Rose al-Yousef, 1965

Like a letter arriving late to its destination, or a message in a bottle found at sea, the (re)discovery of an unpublished manuscript carries a lingering sense of something lost: what might have been had it arrived sooner? In this case, how could this book have influenced Egypt's —or all of Arabic—literary history?

By Nariman Youssef
and MF Kalfat

Lewis Awad (1915-1990), a writer and critic from Minya, was a postgraduate student in Cambridge on a scholarship from Cairo University between 1937 and 1940. *Mudhakkirat Talib Bi'tha* (Diaries of an Overseas Student) is his account of that time and of the journeys there and back.

Not long after World War II broke out, Awad left Cambridge and set off from Tilbury on board a British India Steam Navigation ship, sailing around Scotland in a zigzag across the Atlantic Ocean to Cape Town, then Durban. The journey took forty-five days. There are sightings of sunken battleships, sounds of explosions and fighter jets, detours to avoid German U-boats—the historical context of war is everywhere. But the vividness of the journey comes from more ordinary factors. One is Awad's account of the day-to-day practicalities and frustrations of living on the ship:

> The Madura sailed for a long time in the North Sea, and by the time it docked for supplies, more than a week had passed. All through that time the bar was closed and there was nowhere to buy alcohol or cigarettes. Turns out there's a law that prohibits the sale of those things as long as we are in English water. What a bind! We weren't prepared, so by the second day, cigarettes were running out and we started to borrow off each other. By the third day everyone on board was collecting cigarette butts. By the fourth, it was a shilling for a fag. By the fifth, it was a half crown. Then there were none.
> Eventually the bar opened. The cigarette shortage crisis ended, and the boredom crisis began. Poker it was then, poker all the way from Orkney Islands to the Cap.

Another is the immediacy of the descriptions of surrounding nature:

> At midnight I saw the sun hanging translucent on the western horizon, a bright twilight that shone in the sky and on the sea. For hours the sun hung like this, unmoving, and it was as if the light were emanating from somewhere else, from a magic lamp beyond the world. Eternal twilight and eternal stillness. The rumble of the waves under the Madura wasn't an external noise anymore, but like the buzzing that fills your ear following the sound of a loud explosion. When I focused my attention on the sea and sky and sun, the sound faded and I found myself in a time and space before creation, when time and space were but a thought and there was nothing but endless blue.
> We didn't see the Hebrides, but the birds that filled the horizon let us know they were near. But the stillness was there before the birds and remained there when we'd left them behind. I don't know if the stillness really was that complete, or even noticeable for anyone but me. My imagination might have suppressed the noises in the air or in the water, to recreate the Hebrides that Wordsworth described.

Then there's the ship's demographic. Awad introduces the passengers and divides them into groups: there's the Cambridge group, the London group, the Egyptians, the English, the Irish, the soldiers and the civilians; and once introduced—by name or assigned nickname—they all become characters in daily unfiltered anecdotes, until a sense of the ship's population and the dynamics between them, notably between the English and the Egyptians, begins to take shape:

> From the start, there was a general standoffishness between the Egyptians and the English. An unexplained tension, perhaps triggered by the subtly bullying behaviour on the part of the latter. There are small things you could do to make others feel you were better than them. Without really saying anything. Things that anyone could do. Like when someone asks you the time, you give him a grumpy look. He'd understand and not ask again. [... ...]
> The tension lasted for about three quarters of the trip, but by the end things were fine, sometimes too fine even. [... ...]
> Some were singing and others were dancing or—shall I say—jumping up and down. One Egyptian was holding two whiskies, one in each hand, and an Englishman was bent down drinking from each, while another was riding on an Englishman's back and shouting "Yee-haw!" Sayed Sudan was stuck with a group of drunk-singing English guys so he designated himself their conductor and made them sing silly Egyptian songs.

»مذكرات طالب بعثة«

لويس عَوَض

الناشر: روز اليوسف، سلسلة الكتاب الذهبى، القاهرة، ١٩٦٥، (كتبت فى ١٩٤٢).

Nariman Youssef: I thought I had only the copy you gave me of *Mudhakkirat*, but I've found two in my bookcase instead of one, both 2001 Kitab al-Hilal editions. I know you had been mentioning this book to me for years before I finally read it. Were both copies from you?

MF Kalfat: Only one. Books sometimes lie under our noses until the stars align and it's finally time to pick them up. You could also get so hooked on a book you start giving copies away. Which was the case for me with *Mudhakkirat*. There's also the excitement of having discovered something that, at some point, was nearly lost forever. Awad's manuscript was rejected by the state censors in the 1940s, then his own copy was lost shortly after that, and the book would have never seen the light were it not for a series of serendipities. But even reading it now, a sense of loss remains: whether it might have changed literary history had it appeared closer to the time of its writing. But it didn't, for sheer arbitrary reasons.

NY: Because it didn't get past the censors.

MFK: Yes. The rejection was initially said to be on linguistic grounds, since the book in its entirety is written in spoken Egyptian Arabic (ammeyya). But when Awad pushed back, he was told that he'd forgotten "we're supposed to be England's allies."

NY: The description of a drunk Englishman carrying an Egyptian on his back was cited among the examples of possible anti-British propaganda, unacceptable at a time of war because it "makes the English look bad." Why do you think it might have changed literary history?

———— *"* ————

*Then I wrote often to the sea,
to its sunk rope and its salt bed,
to the large weed mass lipping the bay.*

"The Letter Always Arrives at its Destination,"
Niall Campbell

———— *"* ————

MFK: In Awad's 1965 introduction, he calls the book "an experiment in ammeyya," one of his contributions to the creative writing conundrum of Arabic diglossia.

NY: Which, at the time of publication, he claimed he was no longer invested in.

MFK: He had by then positioned himself as a critic and academic, and this was, as he saw it, an issue for practitioners to resolve.

NY: In other words, only the existence of a body of literary work in ammeyya would make it a literary language.

MFK: By his own definition, Awad's book is a literary/linguistic document that adds to the limited corpus we have of the ammeyya of that time and context, more specifically the register consciously used by a highly educated young Upper-Egyptian Copt intellectual in the 1930s and 40s with an interest in "poetic diction."

NY: One of the things that struck me reading this book was how evocative of a certain past it was. Awad's prose voice reminded me of characters in Egyptian films from the same era. In a way that the more timeless modern standard Arabic doesn't. It also sometimes made me think of Waguih Ghali's characters which, interestingly, only reached us in English.

MFK: We tend to dwell on the notion of whatever is "lost in translation," but I think the literariness of the text is actually what remains in translation. Away from the distractions of the diglossia debate the original has been stuck with. Serious translation, with Walter Benjamin's messianic translator in mind, should be a touchstone, a sieve that not only filters out but also filters in. So that what remains is the more universal, that which is more purely artistic.

NY: But I'm also always interested in the rhythm of the text of the original, and whether—or how—it could be carried into English. I agree with Benjamin to an extent about the essence (das Wesentliche) that is carried by language, but I also strongly believe this essence is as subjective to the translator as the experience of a text could be from reader to reader. In translation, that essence has to be created, not simply carried. Maybe what is always possible to salvaged in translation—along with content value—is the literariness of the text *as experienced by the translator*. But I guess what you're saying is that if there's a strong voice, then there's always a way for it to carry through.

MFK: As it happened, *Mudhakkirat* was published in the same year that brought us Moustafa Mesharrafa's *Qantara Alladhi Kafar* (*Qantara Who Disbelieved*), another book in the short list of works that fall within the boundaries of what is considered—in Richard Jacquemond's sense—"legitimate" literature in Egypt. Then—fast forward to 2018—enters Nadia Kamel's *El-Mawlouda* (*Née*, or *Born As*). Taking these three works together, a cacophony of voices emerges from beneath layers and layers of suppression: of the poor, Copts, communists, daring intellectuals, Jews, women, all speaking their "native language."

NY: What is allowed to happen then is, as Kamel puts it in an interview with Nael el-Toukhy, for "the other" to "come as they are."
MFK: And to come back to life. In pondering the merit of belated publication, Awad uses a language of haunting and the images of ghosts: "I don't usually believe in allowing the ghosts of the past to walk all over my present unchecked, even if they're dressed as art."

NY: But he eventually let himself be persuaded that the ghosts were not just his to banish, that the diaries belonged to a collective intellectual and cultural history.
MFK: Long lost cultures and peoples emerge from a hidden past, triumphant in their indignation, which is made even more striking by the initial silencing.

NY: The ghosts that populate in Awad's *Mudhakkirat* are many: lovers and fellow students and the occasional brief appearance by a political and literary celebrity (e.g. Auden, "with his messy hair and fired-up eyes"). It's a testimony of life at the University of Cambridge—also of longish stays in London and Paris—during historically interesting times, "[a] first-hand account," as Raphael Cormack put it, "by a student who in most literature of the time would play a bit-part."
MFK: Also, the backdrop of WWII, glimpses of late colonialism and anti-colonialist movements, and detailed accounts of the logistics of travel during the war, make it a valuable document of its time, which can be read as both a continuation and subversion of the tradition of the "oriental" intellectual's encounter with "the West."

NY: Then there are the descriptions of Cambridge customs—seen through the amused curiosity of an outsider who wants to learn everything there is to learn—and accounts of everyday encounters and conversations and road trips and student pranks. The book belongs to the tradition of literary accounts of European travels by Arabic intellectuals, which also includes Rifa'a al-Tahtawy, Bayram al-Tunsi, Ahmad Faris Shidyaq, and is perhaps just beginning to get some attention in English.
MFK: One cannot help but think of an English translation

as a belated reparation for the rejection and the risk of disappearance that was caused by British colonial censorship on colonial military grounds. Belated visibility—of texts or the characters in the stories they tell—involves a historical triumph that neither the death of the authors nor the passage of time can completely erase.

NY: Is translation a means to bring more attention to a book?
MFK: State publishing in Egypt is largely a reproduction of stillborn books for the benefit of a few outlets. Works are published into only a lesser degree of obscurity. So an English translation could be an opportunity to finally put things right.

NY: In that case, we could see translation as another reversal of the British colonial censorship, or as a parallel twist of fate to how *Mudhakkirat* finally got to be published in Arabic. When it was recovered, a junior employee in the state censorship department who found it interesting passed it on to a friend, and that friend was a literary enthusiast who, twenty years later, made it public.
MFK: And back to the theme of the sea—in today's world where borders on land and sea make freedom of movement near impossible—the UK's recent track record in rejecting visas of even artists and intellectuals invited by or even work for British institutions is particularly appalling—it would be interesting to bring this journey across into English.

A Sea of Languages

In a Skype conversation that zigzagged across the Mediterranean, *ArabLit Quarterly* editor M Lynx Qualey (in Rabat), talked to Palestinian novelist Adania Shibli (in Berlin) and curator of "Studio Creole" Adam Thirlwell (in London). Shibli recently participated in the debut Studio Creole show, along with authors Alejandro Zambra, Dubravka Ugrešić, Ngugi wa Thiong'o, Patrick Chamoiseau, Sayaka Murata, and Sjón.

Each author wrote a new short story that adhered to two requirements: 1) a first-person narrator, who 2) had a conversation with a stranger. During the show, each author read their story for the audience in its original language: Arabic, Spanish, Croatian, Kikuyu, French, Japanese, or Icelandic. But that's where Thirlwell's project parted ways with the ordinary. At Studio Creole, seven different interpreters listened to the stories and brought them into English. As the authors read their work aloud, the interpreters simultaneously spoke into a microphone. Their words were fed to an actor, who performed each story for an audience of around 300. The show ran for three warm July nights in Manchester.

By M Lynx Qualey

STỤ̈ḌİÖ
ĊRÉŌLE

Images from Manchester International Festival

So the audience is hearing the author and the actor…at the same time?

Adam Thirlwell: The other key piece of tech that's involved in this is what are called bone-conduction headphones. So every member of the audience will be wearing bone-conduction headphones, and these headphones don't go in your ear; they sit on the bone just in front of your ear. They were built for runners, because what it means is that the sound goes through the bones in your head, which means you can hear two things at once, because your ears are still free.

So the rough point we've got is that Adania will be reading in Arabic, and inside the audiences' heads will be Adania's voice, but in the room, they'll be able to hear the live actors speaking in English. And what we've found is that, when that happens, and it works, that it does something very strange to the brain, because it really does make you believe you understand seven different languages. It's so odd; it almost makes you forget that you're listening to a translation, so you kind of just think that you're listening to the Arabic and understanding it.

It's like the opposite of speaking in tongues. It's like listening in tongues. You think: I can speak Japanese now!

Is there less authorial anxiety around a translation that exists only in the moment, and then passes away, rather than a translation that's fixed in place as your work in English forever?

Adania Shibli: The interpreter on the stage is like a reader who translates, but who doesn't work on the text. It's almost like you're inside the act of reading. When you read, you immediately have a certain meaning. It's not like translation, where you go back to the text and you work on it and you work on it. It's really the act of reading.

AT: I think that's also why having the actor is so useful, because the actor basically becomes an image of the reader. In a way, this whole setup almost

becomes a kind of incredibly literalized stage version of what happens when you pick up a book in translation. And it's fascinating to see how the interpreter is having to think: I don't have time to get all of this sentence, so what is the crucial bit in the sentence—and maybe I've missed the crucial bit, and I have to go back.

It's kind of wonderful.

By the time you reach the performance, the interpreter will have done rehearsals. So it's not…entirely spontaneous?

AT: The interpreters will have two or three rehearsals, and then each performance will be the same. Yes, by the time they get to the performance, they'll have heard this text a good few times. But what I've discovered in the workshops we've done is that, although that sounds like they will gradually reach some kind of perfect translation, it's such a demanding task to subject a literary text to this kind of process. We did one workshop in December, where we must've read a very short French story, I think about 20 times in two days, and still, for the interpreter, there would be small nuances that would change, that would drift. Even in that kind of intense situation, with a very short text, it was never a fixed thing.

How did you choose the interpreters for such a demanding task? I was at an event at PalFest in 2013, where China Mieville read a literary text he had recently composed, and I listened to the Arabic through headphones. At a certain point, the interpreter just gave up.

AT: To be honest, this has been much harder than I was imagining. The moment we sat down in the very first workshop, months ago, we realized that it's not really a matter of the interpreter's linguistic competence, although that's part of it, because you have to be absolutely fluent in both languages to be able to do this specific task, in a way that you clearly don't if you're recounting a speech in a conference. But I'd say the two things we've been having a problem with are, first, their capacity to cope with the failure of the project, and also their ability to do a deep, genuinely simultaneous translation. There are languages where people are used to simultaneous, and there are languages where people are used to consecutive translation, and we can't do consecutive because it takes too long.

AS: One of the Arabic interpreters at the workshop felt really on edge, because what he's used to translating is legal and economic conferences or events. And this is also very funny, because it shows you the interests, when it comes to Arabic interpretation.

So when you did the practice workshops, the authors brought their completely finished story.

AT: Yes.

AS: No. I mean, I take a really long time to work on texts. I had almost two thirds of it, and I needed more. Sometimes, when I write, I read aloud. There, when we were at the workshop, I had to read it aloud, and to feel the rhythm, and to do some fine-tuning. And actually, I was also updating the interpreter. It's very interesting, because he was responsive immediately. Usually, when I change something, I'm expecting feedback, but he was like, Yeah, okay, whatever you say.

Your idea, Adam, was that everybody brought a finished story to the workshop.

AT: The workshop, from my perspective, it was in no way to help the writers change their text. It was purely for us to get a sense of how this structure would work.

AS: I think these things—correcting or changing or shifting—are always going to happen.

AT: This is something we talked about in rehearsals. There's now an official version of the text that will end up in this book, but there's no reason we need to stick to it in the live version. If when someone's reading their story, they suddenly just change a sentence—the interpreter doesn't know, the interpreter is this really passive person who just has to interpret what they hear. I quite like the idea that you might throw in an extra sentence out of nowhere.

There's a book coming out? Are each of the texts going to be published bilingually?

AT: It's completely bilingual, yes, so it's got every language. But it's not going to be published in the usual sense—it's only available to audience members. It's not for sale. I did basically have this idea that it would never exist as a text, so my middle ground was that this was a text for the show, and it can't be something that you could buy. I don't want it to exist as a book in its own right.

So people are going to sell them online for $600?

AT: I doubt it, I doubt it.

Back to the show. The authors are also actors?

AT: The authors haven't been asked to act, as it were. For a long time, I did love this idea that you'd just see the authors talking to each other, using the interpreters. The problem really was that it was going to force the authors to be actors. Like all artworks, the practical problems have changed some of the ways in which I've imagined the work. In my very first idea, I did have this image of seven writers from seven different languages using the interpreter. And that the audience could also listen in on this multilingual conversation. I think we will do a very, very tiny version of that, probably right at the end of the show, but it won't be as integral to the show as I initially thought.

AS: In the rehearsals, it was very interesting, because we had this conversation, and I was speaking to Sjon, and he was speaking to me in Icelandic, and I was responding in Arabic. It was beautiful—the possibility of speaking, although you don't know the language of the other. The language becomes something physical. It's not absent, and it's not something going on in your head, like before. The language becomes the sound of it, not the meaning.

AT: And we're quite comfortable with moments of incomprehension. Just having an audience forced to listen to languages they cannot understand—if only for 10 seconds—is an interesting experience.

The Wide Sea

It's no secret that words from the same root in Arabic are related. Yet words with the same root letters, even when in a different order, share astonishing semantic kinship. The letters Ba-Ha-Ra exhibit the concepts of distance, sharpness, being apart, spaciousness, and even generosity.

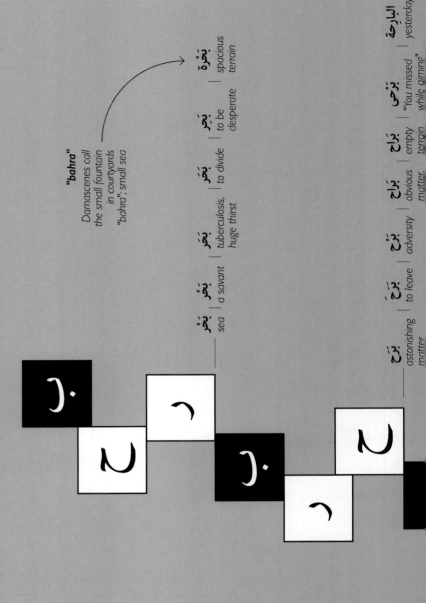

"bahra"
Damascenes call the small fountain in courtyards "bahra", small sea

بَحْر | sea

بَحْر | a savant

بِحْر | tuberculosis, huge thirst

بَحَرَ | to divide

بَحِرَ | to be desperate

بُحْرة | spacious terrain

بَهَرَ | astonishing matter

بُهْر | adversity

بَهَرَ | to leave

بَهْرَة | astonishing matter

حَبَرَ | obvious matter

حَبْر | empty terrain

بَرَحَ | "You missed while qiming"

البَارِحة | yesterday

"habr"
polymath

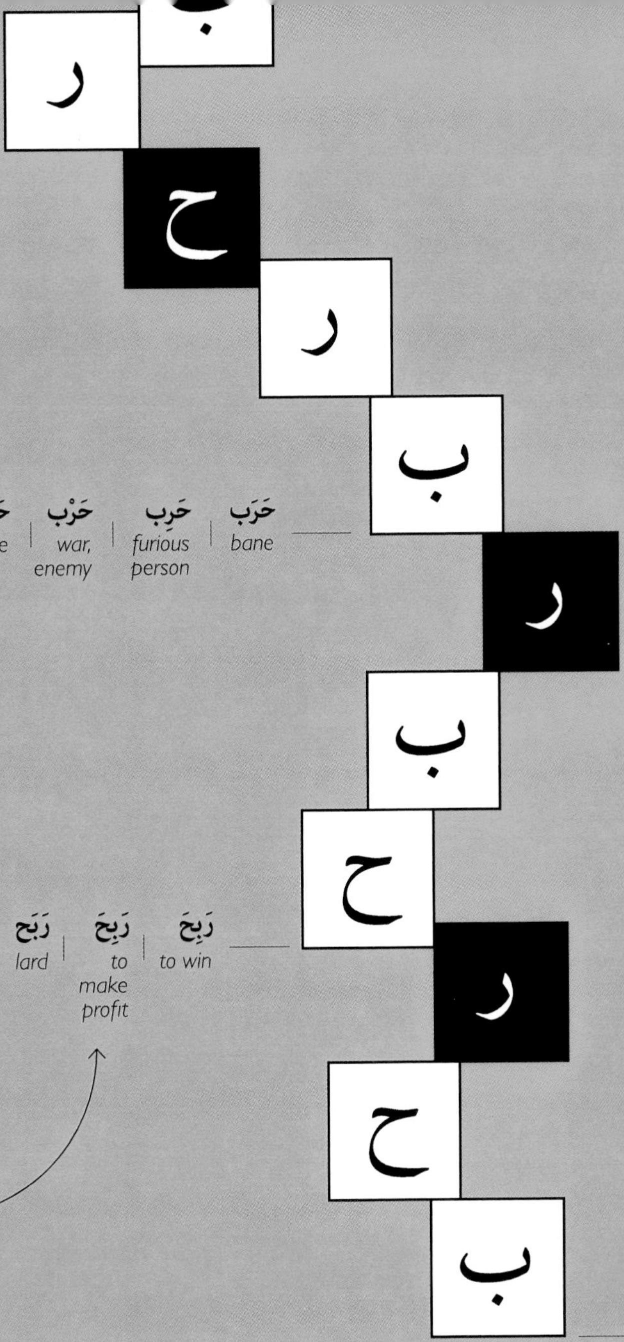

خُبْرَة | prosperity

حِبْر | ink

حَبْر | an imam, a bishop, a rabbi

حَبِرَ | to flourish, to yellow (teeth)

حَبَّرَ | to clarify, to distinguish, to beautify

حَرْبَة | lance

حَرْب | war, enemy

حَرِب | furious person

حَرَب | bane

حَرَّاب | causing conflicts by clandestine or illicit actions

"harba"
is also the
Maghrebi word for
"refrain" which is
called "lazima" in
Standard Arabic

رِبْح | lard

رَبَّحَ | to make profit

رَبِحَ | to win

profit
the excess of
the selling price
of goods over
their cost

Merriam-Webster

رَحُبَ | to become wide or spacious

رَحَّبَ | to welcome

رَحْبَة | courtyard of a mosque

الرُحْضَى | thick rib of the camel

By Hassān Al Mohtasib

Shamar Akhdar

Pickling fresh fennel

This recipe, from the fourteenth-century cookbook *Treasure Trove of Benefits and Variety at the Table*, translated by Nawal Nasrallah, uses ambergris, a treasured ingredient for perfumes and also cooking. In Abu Zayd al-Sirafi's early tenth-century travel book, *Accounts of China and India*, he remarks that people who lived near the coast of the horn of Africa, then known as the Zanj, had trained their camels to scan the shore for ambergris, which might also be found floating on the surface of the sea in lumps the size of a bull.

Although al-Sirafi certainly knew to associate ambergris with whales, he did not know it was a waxy substance exuded by the intestines of sperm whales, usually "as a result of irritation caused by the undigested beaks of cuttlefish or giant squid," according to al-Sirafi's translator Tim Mackintosh-Smith.

By Nawal Nasrallah

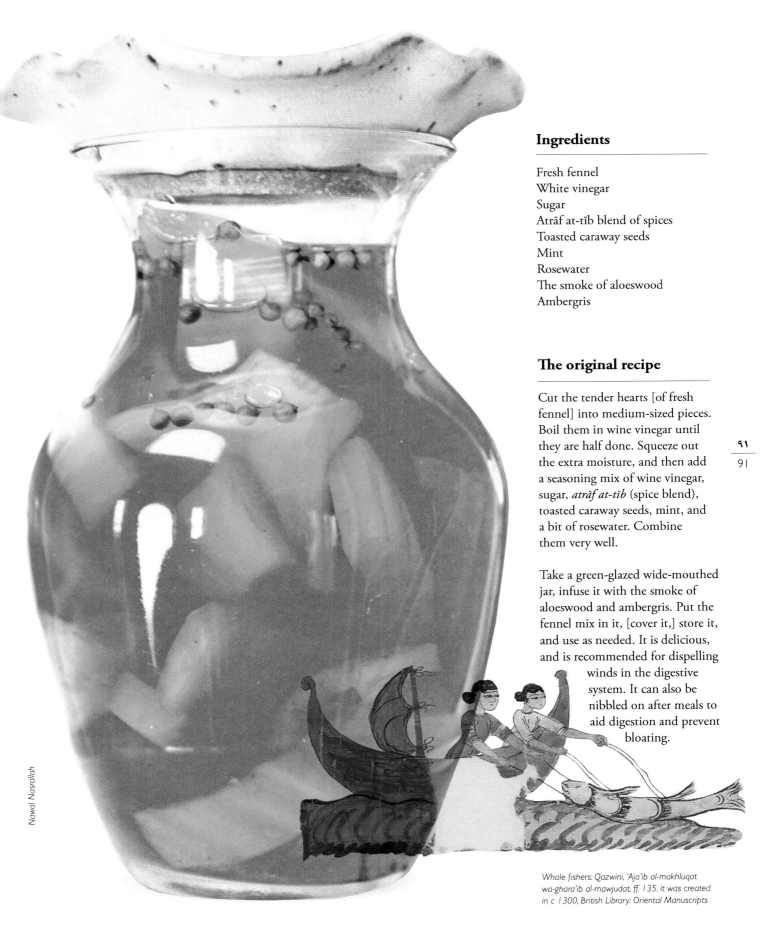

Ingredients

Fresh fennel
White vinegar
Sugar
Atrāf at-tīb blend of spices
Toasted caraway seeds
Mint
Rosewater
The smoke of aloeswood
Ambergris

The original recipe

Cut the tender hearts [of fresh fennel] into medium-sized pieces. Boil them in wine vinegar until they are half done. Squeeze out the extra moisture, and then add a seasoning mix of wine vinegar, sugar, *atrāf at-tīb* (spice blend), toasted caraway seeds, mint, and a bit of rosewater. Combine them very well.

Take a green-glazed wide-mouthed jar, infuse it with the smoke of aloeswood and ambergris. Put the fennel mix in it, [cover it,] store it, and use as needed. It is delicious, and is recommended for dispelling winds in the digestive system. It can also be nibbled on after meals to aid digestion and prevent bloating.

Nawal Nasrallah

Whale fishers: Qazwini, 'Aja'ib al-makhluqat wa-ghara'ib al-mawjudat, ff. 135. It was created in c 1300, British Library: Oriental Manuscripts

Contributors

A

Salim A Al-Abbar is a Libyan author.

Ramy Al-Asheq is a poet, journalist, and curator based in Berlin. He's published five poetry collections in Arabic. Many of his works have been published in anthologies and literary magazines in Bosnian, English, French, German, Kurdish and Spanish.

Lewis Awad (1915-1990) was a journalist, literary critic, historian of ideas and philologist. He did his postgraduate studies at Cambridge and Princeton and, until his academic career was cut short by the 1954 crackdown on pro-democracy figures, taught English Literature at Cairo University.

B

Najwa Binshatwan is a Libyan academic and novelist. She is the author of three novels: *The Horses' Hair* (2005), *Orange Content* (2008), and *The Slave Pens* (2016), which was the first novel by a Libyan to be shortlisted for the International Prize for Arabic Fiction. She was also chosen as one of the Beirut 39, a list of 39 great Arab authors under 40, and won the Banipal Visiting Writer Fellowship in 2018. Several of her short stories have been included in anthologies in English.

D

Emily Drumsta is an Assistant Professor in the Department of Comparative Literature at Brown University. She was the recipient of a 2018 PEN/Heim Award for her translation, *Revolt Against the Sun: The Selected Poetry of Nazik al-Mala'ikah.*

G

Muhammad Lutfi Gumaa was a prolific Egyptian author who wrote and translated novels (including Ulysses) and penned nonfiction on a variety of topics, including folklore, dialect, and Islamic history.

H

Born and raised in Cairo, **Muhammad El-Hajj** is a writer, translator, and digital content creator. His debut collection of short stories, *Nobody Mourns the City's Cats* (2018), won the Sawiris Cultural Foundation's Short Story Prize for emerging writers. He's currently working on his next collection of short fiction.

Russell Harris is an established translator of literary works from French and Arabic.

Sawad Hussain is an ArabLit Quarterly contributing editor, as well as an Arabic translator and litterateur who holds an MA in Modern Arabic Literature from the School of Oriental and African Studies. Some of her recent translations include Saud Alsanoussi's *Mama Hissa's Mice* and a co-translation of Fatima Sharafeddine and Samar Mahfouz Barraj's *Ghady & Rawan.*

J

Essam M Al-Jassim is a writer and translator who graduated from King Faisal University. He lives in Hufof, Saudi Arabia

K

MF Kalfat is an independent cultural worker based in Cairo. He translates, edits, writes, curates film programs, and blogs at mfkalfat.wordpress.com.

Nidal Khalaf has a Master's student in Chemical Engineering from the American University of Beirut (AUB), as well as a freelance rranslator and editor. Nidal's passion for the Arabic language was nurtured at the AUB while he served as Arabic editor for *Outlook*, the university's official newspaper. Currently, Nidal is a Visiting Researcher at the University of Limerick, Ireland.

Ben Koerber is an assistant professor of Arabic in the Department of African, Middle Eastern, and South Asian Languages and Literatures at Rutgers University. He is the translator of Ahmed Naji's *Using Life*, ill. Ahmed Zorkany.

M

Melanie Magidow is the founder of Marhaba Language Expertise, providing Arabic to English translation and other multilingual services. She is also a co-host of the Goodreads MENA Lit Book Group. For more on her malhun projects, see: http://bit.ly/Malhun.

Rawan Maki is a Bahraini, London-based fashion designer and PhD candidate in Fashion Sustainability at the London College of Fashion. The way Rawan approaches sustainability—in both her designs and PhD research—is material, ethical, and social. During her design process, Rawan sketches, writes, and paints. Rawan's PhD research looks at transitioning into sustainability and what that would entail for the Arab world on a material, cultural and socio-political level. In her designs, Rawan combines her environmental engineering background with fashion-design principles and thinks of each piece as a "system," both aesthetically and in terms of zero-waste design principles.

The Iraqi poet **Nazik al-Malaika** was one of the most important Arab poets of the twentieth century. A pioneer of free verse poetry, over the course of a four-decade career, she would publish prolifically and carved out a space for herself between old and new, tradition and innovation, the time-honored and the iconoclastic.

Suneela Mubayi earned her Ph.D. in Arabic literature at NYU, where she completed a thesis on the intersection of classical and modern Arabic poetry. She has translated poems and short stories between Arabic, English, and Urdu, which have been published in Banipal, Beirut39, Jadaliyya, Rusted Radishes and elsewhere. She wishes to re-establish the position of Arabic as a vehicular language of the global South, the role it played for many centuries.

Ahmed Naji is an Egyptian novelist and journalist. He is the author of several books, Rogers, Seven Lessons Learned from Ahmed Makky, Using Life, and The Mystery of the Murdered Mahragan Singer, as well as numerous blogs and other articles. On May 16, 2016, PEN honored Ahmed Naji with the PEN/Barbey Freedom to Write Award recognizing his struggle in the face of adversity for the right to freedom of expression. Ahmed was sentenced to two years in prison after being accused of "violating public modesty" with Using Life. He spent 2016 in prison, and after three years of struggle with the Egyptian legal system, he was able to leave the country and move to Las Vegas with his family.

Hassan Najmi, born in Ben Ahmed in 1960, now resides in Rabat. He is the author of two novels and ten poetry collections. His poetry has been translated into more than ten languages and he has himself translated many poets into Arabic, including Giuseppe Ungaretti, Sophia de Mello Breyner Andresen, Philippe Jaccottet, Yannis Ritsos, and Anna Akhmatova.

Nawal Nasrallah is an independent scholar previously professor of English literature at the universities of Baghdad and Mosul. She has published books and articles on the history and culture of the Middle-Eastern/Arab food, including *Delights from the Garden of Eden: A Cookbook and History of the Iraqi Cuisine* (Equinox Publishing); and two English translations of medieval Arabic cookbooks: *Annals of the Caliphs' Kitchens* and *Treasure Trove of Benefits and Variety at the Table*, both published by Brill.

Taleb Al-Refai is a Kuwaiti author who was born in 1958. He received the State Prize in Literature in 2002 for his novel *The Smell of the Sea* and in 2016 for his novel *Here*, which reached the longlist of the International Prize for Arabic Fiction that year, as did *Najdi* in 2018. He founded *Al-Fonoun* newspaper and the "Al Multaqa Prize for the Arabic Short Story." He has taught creative writing as a visiting professor, presided over the jury of the International Prize for Arabic Fiction, and his fictions have been translated into French, English, Spanish, Chinese, and Turkish.

Wadih Saadeh is a Lebanese-Australian poet. The judges of the 2018 Argana Prize, which Saadeh won, cited his unique contribution to "bringing about a change in the path of the Arab prose poem."

Tópé Salaudeen-Adégòkè is an editor, literary critic and poet from Ibadan, Nigeria. Tópé is the co-publisher of the Nigerian based travel journal, *Fortunate Traveller*. He writes for *Wawa Book Review, Abuja*, and the *African in Words* blog. Some of his essays, poems, creative nonfiction, reviews and interviews have appeared in *Sarabamag, Ake Review, Panorama: Journal of Intelligent Travel, African Writer, Brittle Paper, Nigerian Tribune, The Guardian* and elsewhere. His chapbook of travels across Africa, *Transacting Stories: Markets, People and Place*s was recently published by Invisible Borders Trans-African Photographers Organisation, part of their exhibition 'A Volatile Negotiation Between the Past and Present' at the 2019 AfriCologne Festival, Germany. @LiteraryGansta is his alter ego on Twitter.

Spencer Scoville is Assistant Professor of Arabic at Brigham Young University. His research interests focus on Arabic literature during the Nahda, exploring the roles of literary translation, experimentation, and adaptation on Arabic literature during the long 19th century.

Mbarek Sryfi, a lecturer at the University of Pennsylvania, has translated fiction, poetry, and non-fiction, including three books, two from Arabic and one from French.

T

Levi Thompson is Assistant Professor of Arabic at Colorado University Boulder and is writing a book about modernist poetry across Arabic and Persian.

Y

Nariman Youssef is a translator and writer in English and Arabic. Her literary translations include Inaam Kachachi's *The American Granddaughter* and Donia Kamal's *Cigarette No. 7*.

Z

Yasmine Zohdi is a writer, translator, and the English culture editor at Mada Masr. She holds an MFA in writing from Sarah Lawrence College in New York and is currently working on her first collection of short fiction.

Made in the USA
Monee, IL
07 September 2019